COUNTRY
KITCHEN CLASSICS

D1299525

COUNTRY
KITCHEN CLASSICS

65 TRADITIONAL FARMHOUSE RECIPES

Rustic soups, fish, poultry, game and meat, tarts, cakes, muffins, pies, preserves and relishes, shown in over 245 evocative photographs

SARAH BANBERY

southwater

This edition is published by Southwater
an imprint of Anness Publishing Ltd
Blaby Road, Wigston, Leicestershire LE18 4SE
info@anness.com

www.southwaterbooks.com
www.annesspublishing.com

If you like the images in this book and would
like to investigate using them for publishing,
promotions or advertising, please visit our website
www.practicalpictures.com for more information.

Publisher: Joanna Lorenz
Senior Editor: Felicity Forster
Designer: Design Principals
Cover Design: Jonathan Davison
Recipes: Pepita Aris, Catherine Atkinson, Alex Barker,
    Ghillie Başan, Georgina Campbell, Carla Capalbo,
    Miguel de Castro e Silva, Lesley Chamberlain, Carole
    Clements, Matthew Drennan, Jenni Fleetwood,
    Brian Glover, Christine Ingram, Bridget Jones, Lucy Knox,
    Janet Laurence, Sally Mansfield, Maggie Mayhew, Anna
    Mosesson, Keith Richmond, Rena Salaman, Jennie Shapter,
    Christopher Trotter, Suzanne Vandyck, Laura Washburn,
    Biddy White Lennon, Carol Wilson, Annette Yates
Photographers: Nicki Dowey, Ian Garlick, Amanda Heywood,
    Janine Hosegood, Dave Jordan, William Lingwood, Steve Moss,
    Craig Robertson
Production Controller: Steve Lang

© Anness Publishing Ltd 2012

A CIP catalogue record for this book
is available from the British Library.

Previously published as part of a larger volume,
The Illustrated Practical Book of Country Cooking

NOTES
Bracketed terms are intended for American readers.
For all recipes, quantities are given in both metric and
imperial measures and, where appropriate, in standard cups
and spoons. Follow one set of measures, but not a mixture,
because they are not interchangeable.

Standard spoon and cup measures are level.

1 tsp = 5ml, 1 tbsp = 15ml, 1 cup = 250ml/8fl oz.

Australian standard tablespoons are 20ml. Australian
readers should use 3 tsp in place of 1 tbsp for measuring
small quantities.

American pints are 16fl oz/2 cups. American readers
should use 20fl oz/2.5 cups in place of 1 pint when
measuring liquids.

Electric oven temperatures in this book are for conventional
ovens. When using a fan oven, the temperature will probably
need to be reduced by about 10–20°C/20–40°F. Since ovens
vary, you should check with your manufacturer's instruction
book for guidance.

The nutritional analysis given for each recipe is calculated per
portion (i.e. serving or item), unless otherwise stated. If the
recipe gives a range, such as Serves 4–6, then the nutritional
analysis will be for the smaller portion size, i.e. 6 servings.
Measurements for sodium do not include salt added to taste.

Medium (US large) eggs are used unless otherwise stated.

PUBLISHER'S NOTE
Although the advice and information in this book are
believed to be accurate and true at the time of going to
press, neither the authors nor the publisher can accept any
legal responsibility or liability for any errors or omissions
that may be made nor for any inaccuracies nor for any harm
or injury that comes about from following instructions or
advice in this book.

Main front cover image shows Peach and Blueberry Pie –
for recipe, see pages 70–1.

CONTENTS

Introduction

Country cooking is essentially based on traditional peasant food that has evolved over the centuries. The authentic recipes of the countryside naturally rely on good ingredients and fresh seasonal produce, making use of all the fantastic richness of locally produced food throughout the year. Peasant and country dishes also include many more esoteric foods such as oysters and game which are today regarded as luxury items, but in the past would actually have been classified as poor man's food.

The hard-won knowledge and frugal habits of the country cook, developed with patience over time, are reflected in our 21st-century concerns with the origin and provenance of ingredients. We are beginning to understand that local, fresh, seasonal produce has a better flavour and is far more nutritionally rich than food that is imported from far-flung countries out of season, and this is an area where country recipes shine.

Below *Summer in the country means rich grazing for farm animals and an abundance of produce from the woods, fields and vegetable plot.*

The age-old custom of passing down tried-and-tested traditional family recipes from generation to generation, along with cherished cooking skills, equipment and utensils, means that country food has survived to be appreciated and enjoyed by each new generation of cooks.

The contemporary country kitchen

With a growing interest in cooking seasonally, in using organic produce and the simplest, freshest ingredients, the contemporary country kitchen retains much of what is best about traditional cooking, but with the added blessing of modern equipment, time-saving gadgets and state-of-the-art appliances. Present-day culinary innovations such as pressure cookers and bread machines mean that the busy home cook can now recreate many of the more time-consuming recipes of the past in a fraction of the time, without losing any authentic taste in the finished product. In modern kitchens, it is easier than ever to make the most of all the fresh, high-quality ingredients on which old-style country cooking is based.

Home-made food

Country cooking is simply delicious home-made food using traditional raw materials, without any unnecessary waste. For example, many meat dishes involve long, slow cooking, making use of every possible part of an animal such as the trotters, the head and the offal. This thrifty custom has played a key role in developing some of the best-loved country meat recipes.

An integral part of this style of cooking was preserving food, which was an absolute necessity rather than an indulgence. Home baking and home smoking, along with pickling and salting, and making cheese and butter, were a natural part of living in the country and a matter of pride. Many a country larder contained neat rows of preserved fruit and vegetables in jars, with maybe a ham or some game hanging on a hook and a crock of salted fish ready to be eaten in the cold months of winter. Techniques such as making a rich stock from meat bones or vibrant crab apple jelly from windfall fruits illustrate the inventiveness that characterizes much country cooking.

The seasons

Culinary creativity was very important to the country cook, whose life revolved around the seasons. Traditional recipes tended to be structured around one central ingredient which was in season – spring vegetables tasting wonderful in a delicious soup, or pork as the main ingredient of a raised pie, for example. If there was an abundance of one crop, it was either used fresh in different ways or stored for the cold weather.

Spring could still be a time of year when the cook was largely reliant on preserved foods to support the few early vegetables, while the warm summer months provided plenty of fresh fruits, vegetables and salads from an overflowing and ripe kitchen garden. In the cooler autumn months, the country cook has traditionally relied heavily on wild foods to support the larder and pantry. Game from the fields and woods, as well as a variety of hedgerow fruits and nuts, typically complemented the last of the summer crops. Winter recipes reflect the thriftiness of country cooking, with hearty stews making the most of the root vegetables,

brassicas and dried beans and peas, and using bottled and pickled vegetables from the store cupboard to bulk up meagre winter crops.

Country traditions

The simple act of baking a certain loaf of bread or a special cake for a specific celebration or festival evolved over time to become an indelible part of country tradition. These rituals, treasured and passed down within families, connected people both to the rhythms of the countryside and to the traditions of their local community, marking the passing of the year. Harvest suppers, spiced Christmas drinks, festival sweetmeats and Easter cakes are all concocted from ancient recipes in the country kitchen.

Today, spending time in the kitchen baking a fruit cake, chopping home-grown vegetables to make soup or

Left Baking day was always a regular country tradition, providing a selection of delicious home-made cakes and muffins for the coming week.

Above Home-grown local fruits such as these beautiful peaches and apricots are used in many country recipes, such as a sweet dessert or for making jam.

cooking wonderfully nutritious food from a few simple ingredients reconnects us to the countryside. Even growing a few herbs in pots on the window sill or making your own preserves can give a satisfying feeling of keeping up time-honoured culinary customs.

About the book

The recipes in this book are organized into seven chapters, ranging from simple rustic soups and heart-warming pot roasts to best-loved regional specialities, desserts, cakes, preserves and relishes. Many of the dishes can be prepared ahead of time or slow-cooked all day in traditional fashion, bringing the real taste of the country to your table. The book takes its inspiration from the thrifty methods of the past, to help you make delicious home-made meals that everyone will enjoy.

Soups, appetizers and vegetable dishes

A warming bowl of home-made soup with some crusty bread and a chunk of cheese is a staple lunch or supper, relying, like most country cooking, on fresh ingredients. Seasonal treats such as asparagus and new potatoes are best eaten as fresh as possible, so always seek out local suppliers or enrol in a vegetable box scheme that will give access to ingredients that are currently available.

Country minestrone

The famous Italian country soup is made with small pasta, beans and vegetables, which can include whatever ingredients are at hand from the store cupboard.

Serves 4

45ml/3 tbsp olive oil

115g/4oz pancetta, any rinds removed, roughly chopped

2–3 celery sticks, finely chopped

3 medium carrots, finely chopped

1 medium onion, finely chopped

1–2 garlic cloves, crushed

2 x 400g/14oz cans chopped tomatoes

about 1 litre/1¾ pints/4 cups chicken stock

400g/14oz can cannellini beans, drained and rinsed

50g/2oz/½ cup short–cut macaroni

30–60ml/2–4 tbsp chopped flat leaf parsley, to taste

salt and ground black pepper

shaved Parmesan cheese, to serve

1 Heat the oil in a large pan. Add the pancetta, celery, carrots and onion and cook over a low heat for 5 minutes, stirring constantly, until the vegetables are softened.

2 Add the garlic and tomatoes, breaking them up with a wooden spoon. Pour in the stock. Season to taste and bring to the boil. Half cover the pan, lower the heat and simmer gently for 20 minutes, until the vegetables are soft.

3 Drain the beans and add to the pan with the macaroni. Bring to the boil again. Cover, lower the heat and continue to simmer for about 20 minutes more. Check the consistency and add more stock if necessary. Stir in the parsley and taste for seasoning.

4 Serve hot, sprinkled with plenty of Parmesan cheese.

Per portion Energy 198kcal/833kJ; Protein 15.6g; Carbohydrate 23.3g, of which sugars 3.9g; Fat 5.4g, of which saturates 1.4g; Cholesterol 30mg; Calcium 31mg; Fibre 3.2g; Sodium 224mg.

Summer minestrone

For the warmer months, this colourful and delicious light version of the classic soup is full of summer vegetables and herbs, with new potatoes replacing the pasta.

Serves 4

45ml/3 tbsp olive oil

1 large onion, finely chopped

15ml/1 tbsp sun-dried tomato paste

450g/1lb ripe Italian plum tomatoes, peeled and finely chopped

450g/1lb green and yellow courgettes (zucchini), trimmed and chopped

3 waxy new potatoes, diced

2 garlic cloves, crushed

1.2 litres/2 pints/5 cups chicken stock

60ml/4 tbsp shredded fresh basil

50g/2oz/⅔ cup grated Parmesan cheese

salt and ground black pepper

1 Heat the oil in a large pan, then add the chopped onion and cook gently for about 5 minutes, stirring constantly.

2 Stir in the sun-dried tomato paste, chopped tomatoes, chopped green and yellow courgettes, diced new potatoes and crushed garlic.

3 Mix together well and cook gently for 10 minutes, uncovered, shaking the pan frequently to stop the vegetables sticking to the base.

4 Carefully pour in the chicken stock. Bring to the boil, lower the heat, half cover the pan and simmer gently for 15 minutes or until the vegetables are just tender. Add more stock if necessary.

5 Remove the pan from the heat and stir in the basil and half the cheese. Taste for seasoning. Serve hot, sprinkled with the remaining cheese.

Per portion Energy 201kcal/839kJ; Protein 8.1g; Carbohydrate 18.1g, of which sugars 7.8g; Fat 11.2g, of which saturates 3.4g; Cholesterol 10mg; Calcium 170mg; Fibre 3g; Sodium 138mg.

Autumn pumpkin soup with yogurt

This smooth puréed soup is delicious topped with strained yogurt and melted butter drizzled over the top, but a scattering of crunchy toasted pumpkin seeds make a good garnish too. If pumpkins are not in season, you can use butternut squash instead.

Serves 3–4

1kg/2¼lb prepared pumpkin flesh, cut into cubes

1 litre/1¾ pints/4 cups chicken stock

10ml/2 tsp sugar

25g/1oz/2 tbsp butter, or ghee

60–75ml/4–5 tbsp thick and creamy natural (plain) yogurt

salt and ground black pepper

1 Put the pumpkin cubes into a pan with the stock, and bring the liquid to the boil. Reduce the heat, cover the pan, and simmer for about 20 minutes, or until the pumpkin is tender.

2 Liquidize (blend) the soup in a blender, or use a potato masher to mash the pumpkin flesh. Return the soup to the pan and bring it to the boil again.

3 Add the sugar to the pan and season to taste with salt and pepper. Keep the pan over a low heat while you gently melt the butter or ghee in a small pan over a low heat.

4 Pour the soup into a tureen, or carefully ladle it into individual serving bowls. Swirl a little yogurt on to the surface of the soup and drizzle the melted butter over the top.

5 Serve immediately, offering extra yogurt so that you can enjoy the contrasting burst of sweet and tart in each mouthful.

Per portion Energy 97kcal/406kJ; Protein 2.6g; Carbohydrate 9.3g, of which sugars 8g; Fat 5.8g, of which saturates 3.6g; Cholesterol 14mg; Calcium 104mg; Fibre 2.5g; Sodium 51mg.

Creamy garden pea and mint soup

New peas combined with freshly picked mint from the garden produce a velvety, fresh-tasting soup with a wonderful taste of summer. When peas are out of season, frozen peas will work just as well for this wonderfully green dish.

Serves 6

25g/1oz/2 tbsp butter

1 medium onion, finely chopped

675g/1½lb shelled fresh peas

1.5ml/¼ tsp sugar

1.2 litres/2 pints/5 cups chicken or vegetable stock

handful of fresh mint leaves

150ml/¼ pint/⅔ cup double (heavy) cream

salt and ground black pepper

chopped fresh chives, to serve

1 Melt the butter in a large pan and add the onion. Cook over a low heat for about 10 minutes, stirring occasionally.

2 Add the shelled peas, sugar, stock and half the mint leaves. Cover and simmer gently for 10–15 minutes until the peas are tender.

3 Leave to cool slightly. Add the remaining mint and process or blend until smooth. Return the soup to the pan and season to taste.

4 Stir in the cream and reheat gently without boiling. Serve garnished with chopped chives.

Per portion Energy 121kcal/506kJ; Protein 6.1g; Carbohydrate 9.2g, of which sugars 5.2g; Fat 7g, of which saturates 4.2g; Cholesterol 18mg; Calcium 113mg; Fibre 3g; Sodium 123mg.

Spring vegetables with tarragon

This is almost a salad since the vegetables are only lightly cooked. The bright, fresh flavours are enhanced with the aniseed flavour of tarragon. Serve alongside fish, seafood or chicken.

Serves 4

5 spring onions (scallions)

50g/2oz/¼ cup butter

1 garlic clove, crushed

115g/4oz asparagus tips

115g/4oz mangetouts (snowpeas), trimmed

115g/4oz broad (fava) beans

2 Little Gem (Bibb) lettuces

5ml/1 tsp finely chopped fresh tarragon

salt and ground black pepper

1 Cut the spring onions into quarters lengthways and fry gently over a medium-low heat in half the butter with the garlic.

2 Add the asparagus tips, mangetouts and broad beans. Mix the vegetables gently, making sure they are all well coated in oil.

3 Just cover the base of the pan with water, season, and simmer for a few minutes, until the vegetables are tender.

4 Cut the lettuce into quarters and add the pieces to the pan. Cook for 3 minutes, then, off the heat, swirl in the remaining butter and the tarragon, and serve warm.

Per portion Energy 149kcal/619kJ; Protein 4.7g; Carbohydrate 6.1g, of which sugars 3g; Fat 12g, of which saturates 7.3g; Cholesterol 29mg; Calcium 55mg; Fibre 3.5g; Sodium 89mg.

Fresh green beans and tomato sauce

A standard country summer recipe in Greece made with whichever beans are available, this pretty side dish is most often served with feta cheese, olives and flat bread.

Serves 4

800g/1¾lb green beans, trimmed

150ml/¼ pint/⅔ cup extra virgin olive oil

1 large onion, thinly sliced

2 garlic cloves, chopped

2 small potatoes, peeled and chopped into cubes

675g/1½lb tomatoes or a 400g/14oz can plum tomatoes, chopped

150ml/¼ pint/⅔ cup hot water

45–60ml/3–4 tbsp chopped fresh parsley

salt and ground black pepper

1 If the green beans are very long, cut them in half. Drop them into a bowl of cold water so that they are completely submerged. Leave them to absorb the water for a few minutes. To test if the beans are fresh, snap one in half. If it breaks crisply it is fresh; if it bends rather than breaking, the beans are not fresh.

2 Heat the olive oil in a large pan, add the onion and sauté until translucent. Add the garlic, then, when it becomes aromatic, stir in the potatoes and sauté the mixture for a few minutes.

3 Add the tomatoes and the hot water and cook for 5 minutes. Drain the beans, rinse them and drain again, then add them to the pan with a little salt and pepper to season. Cover and simmer for 30 minutes.

4 Stir in the chopped parsley, with a little more hot water if the mixture is dry. Cook for 10 minutes more, until the beans are very tender. Serve hot with slices of feta cheese, if you like.

Per portion Energy 350kcal/1,448kJ; Protein 6.6g; Carbohydrate 21.9g, of which sugars 13.4g; Fat 26.9g, of which saturates 4g; Cholesterol 0mg; Calcium 121mg; Fibre 7.7g; Sodium 25mg.

Butter-braised lettuce, peas and spring onions

A well-loved French country recipe, this dish is traditionally served with grilled fish or meat.
Try adding shredded fresh mint or substituting mangetouts or sugar snaps for the peas.

Serves 4

50g/2oz/¼ cup butter

4 Little Gem (Bibb) lettuces, halved lengthways

2 bunches spring onions (scallions), trimmed

400g/14oz shelled peas (about 1kg/2¼lb in pods)

salt and ground black pepper

Variations
• Braise about 250g/9oz baby carrots with the lettuce.
• Cook 115g/4oz chopped smoked bacon in the butter. Use 1 bunch spring onions (scallions) and some chopped parsley.

1 Melt half the butter in a wide, heavy pan over a low heat. Add the lettuces and spring onions.

2 Turn the vegetables in the butter, then sprinkle in salt and plenty of ground black pepper. Cover, and cook the vegetables very gently for 5 minutes, stirring once.

3 Add the peas and turn them in the buttery juices. Pour in 120ml/4fl oz/ ½ cup water, then cover and cook over a gentle heat for a further 5 minutes. Uncover and increase the heat to reduce the liquid to a few tablespoons.

4 Stir in the remaining butter. Transfer to a warmed serving dish and serve.

Per portion Energy 161kcal/670kJ; Protein 9.1g; Carbohydrate 15.9g, of which sugars 6.8g; Fat 7.4g, of which saturates 3.7g; Cholesterol 13mg; Calcium 73mg; Fibre 6.5g; Sodium 47mg.

Cauliflower cheese

A mature, strong farmhouse cheddar cheese gives an authentic taste to this simple country classic, or try making this recipe with half cauliflower and half broccoli florets.

Serves 4

1 medium cauliflower

25g/1oz/2 tbsp butter

25g/1oz/4 tbsp plain (all-purpose) flour

300ml/½ pint/1¼ cups milk

115g/4oz mature (sharp) Cheddar or Cheshire cheese, grated

salt and ground black pepper

1 Trim the cauliflower and cut it into florets. Bring a pan of lightly salted water to the boil, drop in the cauliflower and cook for 5–8 minutes or until just tender. Drain and transfer the florets into an ovenproof dish.

2 To make the sauce, melt the butter in a pan, stir in the flour and cook gently, stirring constantly, for about 1 minute (do not allow it to brown). Remove from the heat and gradually stir in the milk. Return the pan to the heat and cook, stirring, until the mixture thickens and comes to the boil. Simmer gently for 1–2 minutes.

3 Stir in three-quarters of the cheese and season to taste. Spoon the sauce over the cauliflower and sprinkle the remaining cheese on top. Put under a hot grill (broiler) until golden brown.

Cook's tip Boost the cheese flavour by adding a little English (hot) mustard to the cheese sauce.

Per portion Energy 318kcal/1318kJ; Protein 17.4g; Carbohydrate 4.4g, of which sugars 3.9g; Fat 25.8g, of which saturates 16.3g; Cholesterol 71mg; Calcium 371mg; Fibre 1.8g; Sodium 453mg.

Irish colcannon

This traditional Irish dish is often served at Hallowe'en with a ring hidden inside it to predict the wedding of the person who finds it. You can use curly kale, cabbage or cavolo nero for a variation. Serve topped with a fried or poached egg, or with a stew or roast.

Serves 6–8

450g/1lb potatoes, peeled and boiled

450g/1lb curly kale or cabbage, cooked

milk, if necessary

50g/2oz/2 tbsp butter, plus extra for serving

1 large onion, finely chopped

salt and ground black pepper

Variation If making this dish for Hallowe'en, slip in a wrapped ring just before serving to your guests.

1 Mash the potatoes. Chop the kale or cabbage, add it to the potatoes and mix. Stir in a little milk if the mash is too stiff.

2 Melt a little butter in a frying pan over a medium heat and add the onion. Cook until softened. Remove and mix well with the potato and kale or cabbage.

3 Add the remainder of the butter to the hot pan. When very hot, turn the potato mixture on to the pan and spread it out. Fry until brown, then cut it roughly into pieces and continue frying until they are crisp and brown. Serve in bowls or as a side dish, with plenty of butter.

Per portion Energy 306kcal/1281kJ; Protein 5.4g; Carbohydrate 40.6g, of which sugars 13.6g; Fat 14.6g, of which saturates 8.8g; Cholesterol 36mg; Calcium 104mg; Fibre 5.9g; Sodium 127mg.

Potatoes roasted with goose fat and garlic

Goose or duck fat gives the best flavour for roasting potatoes. In addition to the garlic, try adding a couple of bay leaves and a sprig of rosemary or thyme to the roasting pan. For a vegetarian version, use a large knob of butter and a splash of olive oil.

Serves 4

675g/1½lb floury potatoes, such as Maris Piper, peeled

30ml/2 tbsp goose fat

12 garlic cloves, unpeeled

salt and ground black pepper

1 Preheat the oven to 190°C/375°F/ Gas 5. Cut the potatoes into large chunks and cook in a pan of salted, boiling water for 5 minutes. Drain well and give the colander a good shake to fluff up the edges of the potatoes. Return the potatoes to the pan and place it over a low heat for 1 minute to steam off any excess water.

2 Meanwhile, spoon the goose fat into a roasting pan and place in the oven until hot, about 5 minutes. Add the potatoes to the pan with the garlic and turn to coat in the fat. Season well with salt and ground black pepper and roast for 40–50 minutes, turning occasionally, until the potatoes are golden and tender.

Per portion Energy 185kcal/778kJ; Protein 2.9g; Carbohydrate 27.2g, of which sugars 2.2g; Fat 7.9g, of which saturates 3.2g; Cholesterol 7mg; Calcium 10mg; Fibre 1.7g; Sodium 19mg.

Asparagus with hollandaise sauce

The asparagus season is short, and this country dish makes the most of its delicate and distinctive flavour. Asparagus can be served simply with melted butter drizzled over the top, but this delicious whisked white wine hollandaise sauce makes it really special.

Serves 4

2 bunches of asparagus

30ml/2 tbsp white wine vinegar

2 egg yolks

115g/4oz butter, melted

juice of ½ lemon

salt and ground black pepper

Cook's tips
• Asparagus should be cooked and eaten as soon as possible, preferably on the day it is picked.
• Make stock with the woody ends of the asparagus rather than throwing them away and add it to vegetable soups or sauces, or use for risotto.

1 Snap off the tough ends of the asparagus. Drop the spears into fast boiling water, cooking for 1–2 minutes until just tender. Test the thickest part of the stalk with a small sharp knife; take care not to overcook.

2 In a pan, bring the vinegar to the boil and bubble until it has reduced to just 15ml/1 tbsp. Remove from the heat and add 15ml/1 tbsp cold water.

3 Whisk the egg yolks into the vinegar and water mixture, then put the pan over a very low heat and continue whisking until the mixture is frothy and thickened.

4 Remove from the heat again and slowly whisk in the melted butter. Add the lemon juice and seasoning to taste. Serve the sauce immediately with the drained asparagus.

Per portion Energy 276kcal/1135kJ; Protein 5.3g; Carbohydrate 2.7g, of which sugars 2.6g; Fat 27.1g, of which saturates 15.9g; Cholesterol 162mg; Calcium 51mg; Fibre 2.1g; Sodium 180mg.

Marinated bean and courgette salad

This bright green, fresh and healthy salad makes the most of a summer glut of courgettes. Add some chopped soft herbs, such as chervil, dill or tarragon, and crumble over fresh ricotta or cubed mozzarella cheese. Serve as an accompaniment to meat and chicken dishes.

Serves 4

2 courgettes (zucchini), halved lengthways and sliced

400g/14oz can flageolet or cannellini beans, drained and rinsed

grated rind and juice of 1 unwaxed lemon

45ml/3 tbsp garlic-infused olive oil

salt and ground black pepper

1 Cook the courgettes in boiling salted water for 2–3 minutes, or until just tender. Drain well and refresh under cold running water.

2 Transfer the courgettes into a bowl with the beans and stir in the oil, lemon rind and juice and some salt and pepper. Chill for 30 minutes before serving.

Per portion Energy 106kcal/444kJ; Protein 5.5g; Carbohydrate 11.9g, of which sugars 3.5g; Fat 4.4g, of which saturates 0.7g; Cholesterol 0mg; Calcium 62mg; Fibre 4.4g; Sodium 228mg.

Fish and shellfish

Steamed, grilled or barbecued, fish and shellfish are the ultimate fast food. More elaborate dishes originate from the practical needs of fisher folk – after selling the prime catch, the leftover small or ugly fish would be included in tasty and filling stews, transforming them into delicious and nutritious meals. Many cultures share the same basic fish recipes, which can be adapted to include whichever fish are available at the time.

Fisherman's soup

Use whichever fish and shellfish you prefer for this tasty main-course soup, which is almost as substantial as a stew. Serve with slices of home-made crusty brown or soda bread.

Serves 6

25g/1oz/2 tbsp butter

1 onion, finely chopped

1 garlic clove, crushed or chopped

1 small red (bell) pepper, seeded and chopped

2.5ml/½ tsp sugar

a dash of Tabasco sauce

25g/1oz/¼ cup plain (all-purpose) flour

about 600ml/1 pint/2½ cups fish stock

450g/1lb ripe tomatoes, skinned and chopped, or 400g/14oz can chopped tomatoes

115g/4oz/1½ cups mushrooms, chopped

about 300ml/½ pint/1¼ cups milk

225g/8oz white fish, such as haddock or whiting, filleted and skinned, and cut into bitesize cubes

115g/4oz smoked haddock or cod, skinned, and cut into bitesize cubes

12–18 mussels, cleaned (optional)

salt and ground black pepper

chopped fresh parsley or chives, to garnish

1 Melt the butter in a large heavy pan and cook the chopped onion and crushed garlic gently in it until softened but not browned. Add the chopped red pepper. Season with salt and pepper, the sugar and Tabasco sauce. Sprinkle the flour over and cook gently for 2 minutes, stirring. Gradually stir in the stock and add the tomatoes, with their juices and the mushrooms.

2 Bring to the boil over medium heat, stir well, then reduce the heat and simmer until the vegetables are soft. Add the milk and bring back to the boil.

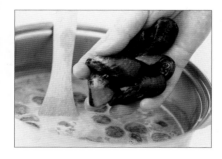

3 Add the fish to the pan and simmer for 3 minutes, then add the mussels, if using, and cook for another 3–4 minutes, or until the fish is just tender but not breaking up. Discard any mussels that remain closed. Adjust the consistency with a little extra fish stock or milk, if necessary. Check the seasoning and serve immediately, garnished with parsley or chives.

Per portion Energy 142kcal/597kJ; Protein 13.9g; Carbohydrate 10.7g, of which sugars 7.1g; Fat 5.2g, of which saturates 2.9g; Cholesterol 36mg; Calcium 84mg; Fibre 1.7g; Sodium 91mg.

Clam, mushroom and potato chowder

This one-pot dish is hearty and substantial enough for supper. The chowder includes sweet, delicately flavoured clams and the earthy flavours of wild and cultivated mushrooms.

Serves 4

48 clams, scrubbed

50g/2oz/¼ cup unsalted (sweet) butter

1 large onion, chopped

1 celery stick, sliced

1 carrot, sliced

225g/8oz assorted wild and cultivated mushrooms

225g/8oz floury potatoes, sliced

1.2 litres/2 pints/5 cups boiling light chicken or vegetable stock

1 thyme sprig

4 parsley stalks

salt and ground black pepper

thyme sprigs, to garnish

1 Place the clams in a large, heavy pan, discarding any that are open. Add 1cm/½in of water to the pan, then cover and bring to the boil.

2 Cook over a medium heat for 6–8 minutes, shaking the pan occasionally, until the clams open (discard any clams that do not open).

3 Drain the clams over a bowl and remove most of the shells, leaving some in the shells as a garnish.

4 Strain the cooking juices into the bowl, add all the cooked clams and set aside.

5 Add the butter, onion, celery and carrot to the pan and cook gently until softened but not coloured.

6 Add the assorted mushrooms and cook for 3–4 minutes until their juices begin to appear. Add the potato slices, the clams and their juices, the chicken or vegetable stock, thyme sprig and parsley stalks.

7 Bring the chowder to the boil, then reduce the heat, cover and simmer for about 25 minutes.

8 Season to taste with salt and pepper, ladle into individual soup bowls, and serve immediately, garnished with thyme sprigs.

Per portion Energy 203kcal/848kJ; Protein 10.8g; Carbohydrate 15.8g, of which sugars 5.2g; Fat 11.2g, of which saturates 6.8g; Cholesterol 60mg; Calcium 66mg; Fibre 2.4g; Sodium 696mg.

Plaice with sorrel and lemon butter sauce

Sorrel is a delicate wild herb that is perfect in this recipe because it does not overwhelm the flavour of the fish. The lemon butter sauce would be good with turbot or brill.

Serves 4

200g/7oz/scant 1 cup butter

500g/1¼lb plaice fillets, skinned and patted dry

30ml/2 tbsp chopped fresh sorrel

90ml/6 tbsp dry white wine

a little lemon juice

1 Heat half the butter in a large frying pan and place the fillets skin side down. Cook briefly, just to firm up, reduce the heat and turn the fish over. The fish will be cooked in less than 5 minutes.

2 Try not to let the butter brown or allow the fish to colour. Remove the fish fillets from the pan and keep warm between two plates. Cut the remaining butter into chunks. Add the chopped sorrel to the pan and stir.

3 Add the wine, then the butter, swirling it in and not allowing the sauce to boil. Stir in a little lemon juice. Serve the fish with the sorrel and lemon butter spooned over, with some crunchy green beans and new potatoes, if you like.

Per portion Energy 494kcal/2047kJ; Protein 25.7g; Carbohydrate 0.5g, of which sugars 0.5g; Fat 43.3g, of which saturates 26.4g; Cholesterol 170mg; Calcium 98mg; Fibre 0.3g; Sodium 501mg.

Kedgeree

A popular breakfast dish in Victorian England, Kedgeree can be made with a variety of smoked fish, and is equally good when served for brunch or at lunchtime.

Serves 4–6

450g/1lb smoked haddock

300ml/½ pint/1¼ cups milk

175g/6oz/scant 1 cup long grain rice

pinch of grated nutmeg and cayenne pepper

50g/2oz/¼ cup butter

1 onion, peeled and finely chopped

2 hard-boiled eggs

salt and ground black pepper

chopped fresh parsley, to garnish

lemon wedges and wholemeal (whole-wheat) toast, to serve

1 Poach the haddock in the milk, made up with just enough water to cover the fish, for about 8 minutes, or until just cooked. Skin the haddock, remove all the bones and flake the flesh with a fork. Set aside.

2 Bring 600ml/1 pint/2½ cups water to the boil in a large pan. Add the rice, cover closely with a lid and cook over a low heat for about 25 minutes, or until all the water has been absorbed by the rice. Season with salt and a grinding of black pepper, and the nutmeg and cayenne pepper.

3 Meanwhile, heat 15g/½oz/1 tbsp butter in a pan and fry the onion until soft and transparent. Set aside. Roughly chop one of the hard-boiled eggs and slice the other into neat wedges.

4 Stir the remaining butter into the rice and add the flaked haddock, onion and the chopped egg. Season to taste and heat the mixture through gently (this can be done on a serving dish in a low oven if more convenient).

5 To serve, pile up the kedgeree on a warmed dish, sprinkle generously with parsley and arrange the wedges of egg on top. Put the lemon wedges around the base and serve hot with the toast.

Variation Instead of the haddock, try leftover cooked salmon.

Per portion Energy 399kcal/1668kJ; Protein 28.9g; Carbohydrate 38g, of which sugars 2.2g; Fat 14.6g, of which saturates 7.6g; Cholesterol 181mg; Calcium 62mg; Fibre 0.5g; Sodium 974mg.

Grilled scallops with bacon

This simple recipe combines succulent scallops and crispy bacon with butter that has just begun to burn but not quite. This gives the dish a lovely nutty smell and a mouth-watering texture. It is delicious served with minted peas and sautéed potatoes.

2 Cut the butter into chunks and put them into a small pan over a low heat.

3 Meanwhile grill (broil) the scallops with the bacon facing up so it protects the meat. The bacon fat will help to cook the scallops. This will take only a few minutes; once they are cooked set aside and keep warm.

4 Allow the butter to turn a nutty brown colour, gently swirling it from time to time. Just as it is foaming and darkening, take off the heat and add the lemon juice. Be warned, it will bubble up quite dramatically.

5 Place the scallops on warmed plates, dress with plenty of chopped fresh parsley and pour the butter over.

Cook's tip Get the scallops on to warmed plates just as the butter is coming to the right colour, then add the lemon juice.

Serves 4

12 rashers (strips) streaky (fatty) bacon

12 scallops

225g/8oz/1 cup unsalted (sweet) butter

juice of 1 lemon

30ml/2 tbsp chopped fresh flat leaf parsley

ground black pepper

1 Preheat the grill (broiler) to high. Wrap a rasher of bacon around each scallop so it goes over the top and not round the side.

Per portion Energy 665kcal/2749kJ; Protein 24.4g; Carbohydrate 2.7g, of which sugars 0.6g; Fat 62g, of which saturates 34.7g; Cholesterol 189mg; Calcium 51mg; Fibre 0.5g; Sodium 1240mg.

Barbecued stuffed sardines

Perfect for summer barbecues, this recipe can also be made with red mullet or trout. Use plump fresh fish and a mixture of fresh herbs. Simply grill, griddle or barbecue the fish, and then serve with extra lemon wedges for squeezing over the top.

Serves 4

15ml/1 tbsp currants

4 good-sized sardines

30ml/2 tbsp olive oil

6 spring onions (scallions),
finely sliced

2–3 garlic cloves, crushed

5ml/1 tsp cumin seeds, crushed

5ml/1 tsp sumac

15ml/1 tbsp pine nuts

1 small bunch flat leaf parsley,
leaves finely chopped

salt and ground black pepper

For basting

45ml/3 tbsp olive oil

juice of 1 lemon

5–10ml/1–2 tsp sumac

1 Prepare the barbecue, if using. Soak four wooden skewers in cold water for 30 minutes. Soak the currants in warm water for about 15 minutes, then drain them.

2 Slit the sardines from head to tail with a sharp knife and remove the backbone by gently massaging the area around it to loosen it. Using your fingers, carefully prise out the bone, snapping it off at each end, while keeping the fish intact. Rinse the fish and pat it dry.

3 Heat the oil in a large, heavy frying pan, stir in the spring onions and cook until soft. Add the garlic, cumin and sumac.

4 Add the pine nuts and currants, stir them into the mixture and fry until they begin to turn golden.

5 Toss in the parsley, and season to taste with salt and pepper. Leave to cool.

6 Heat the grill (broiler), if using. Place each sardine on a flat surface and spread the filling inside each one. Seal by threading the skewers through the soft belly flaps.

7 Mix together the olive oil, lemon juice and sumac, and brush some of it over the sardines.

8 Place the fish on the rack over the hot coals and cook them for 2–3 minutes on each side over a medium heat, basting them with the remainder of the olive oil mixture. Alternatively, grill (broil) the sardines. Serve immediately.

Per portion Energy 265kcal/1098kJ; Protein 16.7g; Carbohydrate 4g, of which sugars 3.1g; Fat 20.3g, of which saturates 3.6g; Cholesterol 0mg; Calcium 90mg; Fibre 0.4g; Sodium 88mg.

Salt cod fritters with garlic aioli

A favourite dish of Portuguese, Spanish and French fishermen, salt cod fritters are delicious when served with an aromatic garlic mayonnaise. If you have any leftover aioli, it can be stirred into a bowl of cold potatoes to make a delicious potato salad.

Serves 6

450g/1lb salt cod

500g/1¼lb floury potatoes

300ml/½ pint/1¼ cups milk

6 spring onions (scallions), finely chopped

30ml/2 tbsp extra virgin olive oil

30ml/2 tbsp chopped fresh parsley

juice of ½ lemon, to taste

2 eggs, beaten

60ml/4 tbsp plain (all-purpose) flour

90g/3½oz/1⅓ cups dry white breadcrumbs

vegetable oil, for shallow frying

salt and ground black pepper

lemon wedges and salad, to serve

For the aioli

2 large garlic cloves

2 egg yolks

300ml/½ pint/1¼ cups olive oil

lemon juice, to taste

1 Soak the salt cod in cold water for 24 hours, changing the water about 5 times. The cod should swell as it rehydrates and a tiny piece should not taste too salty when tried. Drain well.

2 Cook the potatoes, unpeeled, in a pan of boiling salted water for about 20 minutes, until tender. Drain, then peel and mash the potatoes.

3 Poach the cod very gently in the milk with half the spring onions for 10–15 minutes, or until it flakes easily. Remove the cod and flake it with a fork into a bowl, discarding bones and skin.

4 Add 60ml/4 tbsp mashed potato to the flaked cod and beat with a wooden spoon. Work in the olive oil, then gradually add the remaining potato. Beat in the remaining spring onions and parsley. Season with lemon juice and pepper to taste – it may need a little salt. Beat in 1 egg, then chill until firm.

5 Shape the mixture into 12 round cakes. Coat them in flour, then dip in the remaining egg and coat with the breadcrumbs. Chill until ready to fry.

6 Meanwhile, make the aioli. Place the garlic and a good pinch of salt in a mortar and pound to a paste with a pestle. Using a small whisk or a wooden spoon, gradually work in the egg yolks.

7 Add the olive oil, a drop at a time, until half is incorporated. When the sauce is as thick as soft butter, beat in 5–10ml/ 1–2 tsp lemon juice, then continue adding oil until the aioli is very thick. Adjust the seasoning, adding lemon juice to taste.

8 Heat 2cm/¾in depth of oil in a frying pan. Add the fritters and cook over a medium-high heat for 4 minutes. Turn over and cook for a further 4 minutes on the other side, until crisp and golden. Drain on kitchen paper, then serve with the aioli, lemon wedges and salad leaves.

Per portion Energy 653kcal/2721kJ; Protein 32.7g; Carbohydrate 28.1g, of which sugars 4.2g; Fat 46.4g, of which saturates 7.6g; Cholesterol 178mg; Calcium 123mg; Fibre 1.4g; Sodium 472mg.

Maryland crab cakes with tartare sauce

One of the most famous American country dishes, these crab cakes are a modern version of Baltimore crab cakes. The tasty white crab meat is coated in breadcrumbs and fried.

Serves 4

675g/1½lb fresh crab meat

1 egg, beaten

30ml/2 tbsp mayonnaise

15ml/1 tbsp Worcestershire sauce

15ml/1 tbsp sherry

30ml/2 tbsp finely chopped
fresh parsley

15ml/1 tbsp finely chopped
fresh chives

salt and ground black pepper

45ml/3 tbsp olive oil

For the sauce

1 egg yolk

15ml/1 tbsp white wine vinegar

30ml/2 tbsp Dijon-style mustard

250ml/8fl oz/1 cup vegetable oil

30ml/2 tbsp fresh lemon juice

20g/¾oz/¼ cup finely chopped
spring onions (scallions)

30ml/2 tbsp chopped drained capers

few finely chopped sour dill pickles

60ml/4 tbsp finely chopped
fresh parsley

1 Pick over the crab meat, removing any shell or cartilage.

2 In a mixing bowl, combine the beaten egg with the mayonnaise, Worcestershire sauce, sherry and herbs. Season with salt and pepper. Gently fold in the crab meat. Divide the mixture into eight portions and gently form each one into an oval cake. Place on a baking sheet between layers of baking parchment and chill for 1 hour.

3 Make the sauce. In a bowl, beat the egg yolk. Add the vinegar, mustard and salt and pepper, and whisk for 10 seconds. Whisk in the oil in a slow, steady stream.

4 Add the lemon juice, spring onions, capers, pickles and parsley and mix well. Check the seasoning. Cover and chill for at least 30 minutes.

5 Preheat the grill (broiler). Brush the crab cakes with the olive oil. Place on an oiled baking sheet, in one layer.

6 Grill (broil) 15cm/6in from the heat until golden brown, about 5 minutes on each side. Serve the crab cakes hot with the tartare sauce.

Variation You can use defrosted frozen or canned crab meat instead.

Per portion Energy 710kcal/2934kJ; Protein 33.8g; Carbohydrate 1.9g, of which sugars 1.7g; Fat 62.6g, of which saturates 8.1g; Cholesterol 225mg; Calcium 234mg; Fibre 0.2g; Sodium 1249mg.

Poultry and game

Chicken and other poultry are among the most popular and versatile meats, and they can be prepared in a huge variety of ways, from a simple roasted bird to delicious rustic pâtés. In the past, game was a seasonal meat available only at certain times of the year, but it is now possible to obtain a wide variety of game all year round. It is, however, still rewarding to cook game with traditional seasonal ingredients.

Lemon and garlic pot roast chicken

Pot roasting is at the heart of rustic cooking. Easy to prepare and slow cooked, this is a great family dish. Serve with baked rice, mashed potatoes or thick bread.

Serves 4

30ml/2 tbsp olive oil

25g/1oz/2 tbsp butter

175g/6oz/1 cup smoked lardons, or roughly chopped streaky (fatty) bacon

8 garlic cloves, peeled

4 onions, quartered

10ml/2 tsp plain (all-purpose) flour

600ml/1 pint/2½ cups chicken stock

2 lemons, thickly sliced

45ml/3 tbsp chopped fresh thyme

1 chicken, about 1.3–1.6kg/3–3½lb

2 x 400g/14oz cans flageolet, cannellini or haricot (navy) beans, drained and rinsed

salt and ground black pepper

3 Bring to the boil, stirring constantly until thickened, then place the chicken on top. Season well. Transfer the casserole to the oven. Cook for 1 hour, basting the chicken once or twice during cooking to ensure it stays moist.

4 Baste the chicken again. Stir the beans into the casserole and return it to the oven for a further 30 minutes, or until the chicken is cooked through and tender. Carve the chicken into thick slices and serve with the beans.

1 Preheat the oven to 190°C/375°F/ Gas 5. Heat the oil and butter in a flameproof casserole that is large enough to hold the chicken with a little room around the sides. Add the lardons and cook until golden. Remove with a slotted spoon and drain on kitchen paper.

2 Add the garlic and onions and brown over a high heat. Stir in the flour, then the stock. Return the lardons to the pan with the lemon, thyme and seasoning.

Per portion Energy 887kcal/3696kJ; Protein 62.5g; Carbohydrate 45.5g, of which sugars 12.9g; Fat 51.7g, of which saturates 16g; Cholesterol 256mg; Calcium 187mg; Fibre 13.9g; Sodium 1519mg.

Chicken baked with forty cloves of garlic

Don't be put off by the amount of garlic in this traditional dish. The garlic heads become soft, sweet and fragrant when cooked, and impart a mouth-watering aroma.

Serves 4–5

5–6 whole heads of garlic

15g/½oz/1 tbsp butter

45ml/3 tbsp olive oil

1.8–2kg/4–4½lb chicken

150g/5oz/1¼ cups plain (all-purpose) flour, plus 5ml/1 tsp

75ml/5 tbsp white port, Pineau de Charentes or other white, fortified wine

2–3 fresh tarragon or rosemary sprigs

30ml/2 tbsp crème fraîche

few drops of lemon juice

salt and ground black pepper

1 Separate three of the heads of garlic into cloves and peel. Remove the first layer of papery skin from the remaining heads of garlic and leave whole. Preheat the oven to 180°C/350°F/Gas 4.

2 Heat the butter and 15ml/1 tbsp of the olive oil in a flameproof casserole that is just large enough to take the chicken and garlic. Add the chicken and cook over a medium heat, turning frequently, for 10 minutes, until it is browned all over. Sprinkle in 5ml/1 tsp flour and cook for 1 minute. Add the port or wine. Tuck in the whole heads of garlic and the peeled cloves with the herb sprigs.

3 Pour the remaining oil over the chicken and season to taste with salt and pepper. Rub all over to coat.

4 Mix the main batch of flour with enough water to make a firm dough. Roll it out into a long sausage and press around the rim of the casserole, then press on the lid, folding the dough up and over it to create a tight seal. Cook in the oven for 1½ hours.

5 To serve, lift off the lid to break the seal and remove the chicken and whole garlic to a serving platter and keep warm. Remove and discard the herb sprigs, then place the casserole on the hob and whisk to combine the garlic cloves with the juices. Add the crème fraîche and a little lemon juice to taste. Process the sauce in a food processor or blender if a smoother result is required. Serve the garlic purée with the chicken.

Per portion Energy 787kcal/3276kJ; Protein 51.3g; Carbohydrate 33.2g, of which sugars 1g; Fat 50.6g, of which saturates 14.5g; Cholesterol 248mg; Calcium 77mg; Fibre 2.2g; Sodium 212mg.

Puff pastry chicken pies

These versatile little pies can be filled with different kinds of meat. Although chicken is the most popular, they are also good with a mixture of game and chicken, or with fish or shellfish. They make a tempting afternoon snack, or you could have two or three of them, either hot or cold, with a refreshing salad for a delicious light lunch.

Makes about 12

1 chicken, weighing 1.6–2kg/3½–4½lb

45ml/3 tbsp olive oil

1 sausage, weighing about 250g/9oz

150g/5oz bacon

1 garlic clove

10 black peppercorns

1 onion stuck with 2 cloves

1 bunch of parsley, chopped

4 thyme or marjoram sprigs

juice of 1 lemon or 60ml/4 tbsp white wine vinegar

butter, for greasing

500g/1¼lb puff pastry, thawed if frozen

plain (all-purpose) flour, for dusting

2 egg yolks, lightly beaten

salt

1 Cut the chicken into pieces. Heat the oil in a large, heavy pan. Add the chicken pieces and cook over a medium-low heat, turning occasionally, for about 10 minutes, until golden brown on all sides.

2 Add the sausage, bacon, garlic, peppercorns, onion, parsley, thyme and lemon juice or vinegar. Pour in enough water to cover and bring to the boil. Lower the heat, cover and simmer for 1–1½ hours, until tender.

3 Remove all the meat from the stock with a slotted spoon. Then return the stock to the heat and cook, uncovered, until slightly reduced. Strain the stock into a bowl and season with salt to taste.

4 Remove and discard the chicken skin and bones and cut the meat into small pieces. Cut the sausage and bacon into small pieces. Mix all the meat together. Preheat the oven to 200°C/400°F/Gas 6. Grease a 12-cup muffin tin (pan) with butter.

5 Roll out the pastry thinly on a lightly floured surface and stamp out 12 rounds with a 7.5cm/3in cutter.

6 Gather the trimmings together and roll out thinly again, then stamp out 12 rounds with a 6cm/2½in cutter. Place the larger rounds in the cups of the prepared tin, pressing the pastry to the side with your thumb, and divide the meat among them.

7 Spoon in a little of the stock, then brush the edges with beaten egg yolk and cover with the smaller rounds, pinching the edges to seal.

8 Brush the remaining egg yolk over the top to glaze and make a small hole in the centre of each pie with a wooden cocktail stick (toothpick).

9 Bake for 15–25 minutes, until golden brown. Remove from the oven and leave to cool before serving.

Variation You can use the following dough as an alternative to puff pastry. Sift 500g/1¼lb/5 cups plain (all-purpose) flour into a bowl and make a well in the centre. Add 5 eggs and about 150g/5oz/⅔ cup of the leftover chicken fat to the well and mix together, adding some stock if necessary. Blend well, then shape the dough into a ball and leave to rest, wrapped in clear film (plastic wrap), for 30 minutes before rolling out.

Per pie Energy 368kcal/1534kJ; Protein 24.5g; Carbohydrate 18.3g, of which sugars 1.2g; Fat 22.8g, of which saturates 4.3g; Cholesterol 109mg; Calcium 44mg; Fibre 0.2g; Sodium 547mg.

Country duck pâté with redcurrants

Depending on availability, chicken or duck livers can be used interchangeably to make this lovely country appetizer. The tart flavours and pretty colour and texture of the tiny red berries complement the rich pâté perfectly. This recipe is easy to prepare and the pâté keeps for about a week in the refrigerator if the butter seal is not broken.

Serves 4–6

1 onion, finely chopped

1 large garlic clove, crushed

115g/4oz/½ cup butter

225g/8oz duck livers

10–15ml/2–3 tsp chopped fresh mixed herbs, such as parsley, thyme or rosemary

15–30ml/1–2 tbsp brandy

bay leaf (optional)

50–115g/2–4oz/¼ –½ cup clarified butter, or melted unsalted (sweet) butter

salt and ground black pepper

a sprig of flat leaf parsley, to garnish

For the redcurrant sauce

30ml/2 tbsp redcurrant jelly

15–30ml/1–2 tbsp port

30ml/2 tbsp redcurrants

For the Melba toast

8 slices white bread, crusts removed

1 Cook the onion and garlic in 25g/1oz/2 tbsp of the butter in a pan over gentle heat, until just turning colour.

2 Trim the duck livers. Add to the pan with the herbs and cook together for about 3 minutes, or until the livers have browned on the outside but are still pink in the centre. Allow to cool.

3 Dice the remaining butter, then process the liver mixture in a food processor, gradually working in the cubes of butter by dropping them down the chute on to the moving blades, to make a smooth purée.

4 Add the brandy, then check the seasoning and transfer to a 450–600ml/½–1 pint/scant 2 cups dish. Lay a bay leaf on top if you wish, then seal the pâté with clarified or unsalted butter. Cool, and then chill in the refrigerator until required.

5 To make the redcurrant sauce, put the redcurrant jelly, port and redcurrants into a small pan and bring gently to boiling point. Simmer for about 10 minutes to make a rich consistency. Leave to cool.

6 To make the Melba toast, toast the bread on both sides, then carefully slice each piece of toast vertically to make 16 very thin slices.

7 Place each piece of toast, with the untoasted side up, on a grill (broiler) rack and grill (broil) until browned. (The toast can then be stored in an airtight container for a few days, then warmed through to crisp up again just before serving.)

8 Serve the chilled pâté garnished with parsley and accompanied by Melba toast or toasted slices of brioche and the redcurrant sauce.

Per portion Energy 794kcal/3312kJ; Protein 101.3g; Carbohydrate 11.3g, of which sugars 9.9g; Fat 36.8g, of which saturates 19g; Cholesterol 2213mg; Calcium 73mg; Fibre 1.3g; Sodium 608mg.

Duck with damson ginger sauce

Wild damsons or plums have a sharp taste that make a lovely fruity sauce to serve with these simple and quick-to-cook pan-fried duck breasts. This delicious sauce would also be good with other rich meats such as venison, pheasant or goose.

Serves 4

250g/9oz fresh damsons

5ml/1 tsp ground ginger

45ml/3 tbsp sugar

10ml/2 tsp wine vinegar or sherry vinegar

4 duck breast portions

15ml/1 tbsp oil

salt and ground black pepper

1 Put the damsons in a pan with the ginger and 45ml/3 tbsp water. Bring to the boil, cover and simmer gently for about 5 minutes, or until the fruit is soft. Stir frequently and add a little extra water if the fruit looks as if it is drying out or sticking to the bottom of the pan.

2 Stir in the sugar and vinegar. Press the mixture through a sieve (strainer) to remove stones (pits) and skin. Taste the sauce and add more sugar (if necessary) and seasoning to taste.

3 Meanwhile, with a sharp knife, score the fat on the duck breast portions in several places without cutting into the meat. Brush the oil over both sides of the duck. Sprinkle a little salt and pepper on the fat side only.

4 Preheat a griddle pan or heavy frying pan. When hot, add the duck breast portions, skin side down, and cook over medium heat for about 5 minutes or until the fat is evenly browned and crisp.

5 Turn over and cook the meat side for 4–5 minutes. Lift out and leave to rest for 5–10 minutes.

6 Slice the duck on the diagonal and serve with the sauce.

Cook's tip Both the duck and the sauce are good served cold too. Serve with simple steamed vegetables, crisp salads or in sandwiches.

Per portion Energy 275kcal/1157kJ; Protein 29.9g; Carbohydrate 17.5g, of which sugars 17.5g; Fat 12.5g, of which saturates 2.4g; Cholesterol 165mg; Calcium 39mg; Fibre 1.1g; Sodium 167mg.

Roast young grouse with rowanberries

As with venison, rowan jelly goes well with this meat. Young grouse can be identified by their pliable breastbone, legs and feet, and their claws will be sharp. They have very little fat, so bacon is used here to protect the breasts during the initial roasting.

Serves 2

2 young grouse

6 rashers (strips) bacon

2 sprigs of rowanberries
or 1 lemon, quartered, plus
30ml/2 tbsp extra rowanberries
(optional)

50g/2oz/¼ cup butter

150ml/¼ pint/⅔ cup red wine

150ml/¼ pint/⅔ cup water

5ml/1 tsp rowan jelly

salt and ground black pepper

1 Preheat the oven to 200°C/400°F/ Gas 6. Wipe the grouse with kitchen paper and place in a roasting pan. Lay the bacon over the breasts.

2 If you have rowanberries, place one sprig in the cavity of each grouse as well as a little butter. Otherwise put a lemon quarter in each cavity.

3 Roast the grouse in the preheated oven for 10 minutes, then remove the bacon and pour in the wine. Return to the oven for 10 minutes.

4 Baste the birds with the juices and cook for a further 5 minutes. Remove the birds from the pan and keep warm. Add the water and rowan jelly to the pan and simmer gently until the jelly melts. Strain into another pan, add the rowanberries, if using, and simmer until the sauce just begins to thicken. Season with salt and ground black pepper.

Variation If rowanberries are hard to find, you can replace them with dried cranberries or sour cherries, which will give a similar result.

Per portion Energy 423kcal/1763kJ; Protein 43.8g; Carbohydrate 1.5g, of which sugars 1.5g; Fat 24g, of which saturates 10.8g; Cholesterol 51mg; Calcium 43mg; Fibre 0g; Sodium 902mg.

Pheasant and wild mushroom ragoût

This rich and delicious way to prepare pheasant uses shallots, garlic cloves, port and a mixture of wild mushrooms for a good variety of flavour and texture.

Serves 4

4 pheasant breasts, skinned

15ml/1 tbsp oil

12 shallots, halved

2 garlic cloves, crushed

75g/3oz wild mushrooms, sliced

75ml/2½fl oz/⅓ cup port

150ml/¼ pint/⅔ cup chicken stock

sprigs of fresh parsley and thyme

1 bay leaf

grated rind of 1 lemon

200ml/7fl oz/scant 1 cup double (heavy) cream

salt and ground black pepper

1 Dice and season the pheasant breasts. Heat the oil in a heavy pan and colour the pheasant meat quickly. Remove from the pan and set aside.

2 Add the halved shallots to the pan, fry quickly to colour a little, then add the crushed garlic and sliced wild mushrooms. Reduce the heat and cook gently for 5 minutes.

3 Pour the port and stock into the pan and add the herbs and lemon rind. Reduce the liquid a little. When the shallots are nearly cooked, add the cream, reduce to thicken, then return the meat. Allow to cook for a few minutes before serving.

Cook's tip Serve with pilaff rice: fry a chopped onion, stir in 2.5cm/1in cinnamon stick, 2.5ml/½ tsp crushed cumin seeds, 2 crushed cardamom pods, a bay leaf and 5ml/1 tsp turmeric. Add 225g/8oz/generous 1 cup long grain rice. Stir until well coated. Pour in 600ml/1 pint/2½ cups boiling water, cover, then simmer gently for 15 minutes. Transfer to a serving dish, cover with a dish towel and leave for 5 minutes.

Per portion Energy 530kcal/2200kJ; Protein 34.1g; Carbohydrate 7.4g, of which sugars 5.9g; Fat 33g, of which saturates 20.2g; Cholesterol 69mg; Calcium 91mg; Fibre 1.1g; Sodium 114mg.

Grouse with orchard fruit stuffing

In the late summer and autumn, when grouse are in season, orchard fruits such as apples, plums and pears make a perfect stuffing. Try serving with creamy mashed potatoes.

Serves 2

juice of ½ lemon

2 young grouse

50g/2oz/¼ cup butter

4 Swiss chard leaves

50ml/2fl oz/¼ cup Marsala

salt and ground black pepper

For the stuffing

2 shallots, finely chopped

1 tart cooking apple, peeled, cored and chopped

1 pear, peeled, cored and chopped

2 plums, halved, stoned (pitted) and chopped

large pinch of mixed (apple pie) spice

Cook's tip In this recipe, the birds are steamed rather than boiled, so it is important that the casserole has a heavy base and a tight-fitting lid, otherwise the liquid may evaporate and the chard will burn on the base of the pan.

1 Sprinkle the lemon juice over the grouse and season well. Melt half the butter in a flameproof casserole, add the grouse and cook for 10 minutes, or until browned. Use tongs to remove the grouse from the casserole and set aside.

2 Add the shallots to the fat remaining in the casserole and cook until softened but not coloured. Add the apple, pear, plums and mixed spice, and cook for about 5 minutes, or until the fruits are just beginning to soften. Remove the casserole from the heat and spoon the hot fruit mixture into the body cavities of the birds, filling them well.

3 Truss the birds neatly with string. Smear the remaining butter over the birds and wrap them in the chard leaves, then replace them in the casserole.

4 Pour in the Marsala and heat until simmering. Cover tightly and simmer for 20 minutes, or until the birds are tender, taking care not to overcook them. Leave to rest in a warm place for about 10 minutes before serving.

Per portion Energy 508kcal/2121kJ; Protein 46.9g; Carbohydrate 19.5g, of which sugars 18.7g; Fat 24.3g, of which saturates 13.8g; Cholesterol 53mg; Calcium 185mg; Fibre 4.2g; Sodium 406mg.

Raised game pie

The perfect picnic food traditionally taken on country shoots, this stylish dish makes a spectacular centrepiece when baked in a fluted raised pie mould. The hot water crust pastry is very easy to make, and the pie can be served with piccalilli and pickled onions.

Serves 10

25g/1oz/2 tbsp butter

1 onion, finely chopped

2 garlic cloves, finely chopped

900g/2lb mixed boneless game meat, such as skinless pheasant and/or pigeon breast, venison and rabbit, diced

30ml/2 tbsp chopped mixed fresh herbs such as parsley, thyme and marjoram

salt and ground black pepper

For the pâté

50g/2oz/¼ cup butter

2 garlic cloves, finely chopped

450g/1lb chicken livers, rinsed, trimmed and chopped

60ml/4 tbsp brandy

5ml/1 tsp ground mace

For the hot water crust pastry

675g/1½lb/6 cups strong plain (all-purpose) flour

5ml/1 tsp salt

115ml/3½fl oz/scant ½ cup milk

115ml/3½fl oz/scant ½ cup water

115g/4oz/½ cup lard, diced

115g/4oz/½ cup butter, diced

beaten egg, to glaze

For the jelly

300ml/½ pint/1¼ cups game or beef consommé

2.5ml/½ tsp powdered gelatine

1 Melt the butter in a small pan until foaming, then add the onion and garlic, and cook until softened but not coloured. Remove from the heat and mix with the diced game meat and the chopped mixed herbs. Season well, cover and chill.

2 To make the pâté, melt the butter in a pan until foaming. Add the garlic and chicken livers and cook until the livers are just browned. Remove the pan from the heat and stir in the brandy and mace. Purée the mixture in a blender or food processor until smooth, then set aside and leave to cool.

3 To make the pastry, sift the flour and salt into a bowl and make a well in the centre. Place the milk and water in a pan. Add the lard and butter and heat gently until melted, then bring to the boil and remove from the heat as soon as the mixture begins to bubble. Pour the hot liquid into the well in the flour and beat until smooth. Cover and leave until cool enough to handle.

4 Preheat the oven to 200°C/400°F/Gas 6. Roll out two-thirds of the pastry and use to line a 23cm/9in raised pie mould. Spoon in half the game mixture and press it down evenly. Add the pâté, then top with the remaining game.

5 Roll out the remaining pastry to form a lid. Brush the edge of the pastry lining the mould with water and cover the pie with the lid. Trim off any excess. Pinch the edges together to seal. Make two holes in the centre of the lid and glaze with egg. Use pastry trimmings to roll out leaves to garnish the pie. Brush with egg.

6 Bake the pie for 20 minutes, cover with foil and cook for a further 10 minutes. Reduce the oven temperature to 150°C/300°F/Gas 2. Glaze the pie again with beaten egg and cook for a further 1½ hours, keeping the top covered loosely with foil.

7 Remove the pie from the oven and leave to stand for 15 minutes. Increase the oven temperature to 200°C/400°F/Gas 6. Stand the mould on a baking sheet and remove the sides. Glaze the sides of the pie with beaten egg and cover the top with foil, then cook for a final 15 minutes to brown the sides. Cool completely, then chill the pie overnight.

8 For the jelly, heat the game or beef consommé in a small pan until just starting to bubble, whisk in the gelatine until dissolved and leave to cool until just setting. Using a small funnel, carefully pour the jellied consommé into the holes in the pie. Chill. This pie will keep in the refrigerator for up to 3 days.

Per portion Energy 731kcal/3058kJ; Protein 44g; Carbohydrate 54.3g, of which sugars 2.5g; Fat 32g, of which saturates 17.9g; Cholesterol 223mg; Calcium 163mg; Fibre 2.3g; Sodium 444mg.

Guinea fowl and spring vegetable ragoût

Equally delicious when made with chicken or rabbit, this light stew makes the best of spring vegetables, including tender baby leeks. Finish with plenty of chopped parsley.

Serves 4

45ml/3 tbsp olive oil

115g/4oz pancetta, cut into lardons

30ml/2 tbsp plain (all-purpose) flour

2 × 1.2–1.6kg/2½–3½lb guinea fowl, each jointed in 4 portions

1 onion, chopped

1 head of garlic, separated into cloves and peeled

1 bottle dry white wine

fresh thyme sprig

1 fresh bay leaf

a few parsley stalks

250g/9oz baby carrots

250g/9oz baby turnips

6 slender leeks, cut into 7.5cm/3in lengths

250g/9oz shelled peas

15ml/1 tbsp French herb mustard

15g/½oz flat leaf parsley, chopped

15ml/1 tbsp chopped fresh mint

salt and ground black pepper

1 Heat 30ml/2 tbsp of the oil in a large frying pan and cook the pancetta over a medium heat until lightly browned, stirring occasionally. Remove the pancetta from the pan and set aside.

2 Season the flour with salt and pepper and toss the guinea fowl portions in it. Fry the portions in the oil remaining in the pan until they are browned on all sides. Transfer to a flameproof casserole. Preheat the oven to 180°C/350°F/Gas 4. Add the remaining oil to the pan and cook the onion gently until soft.

3 Add the garlic to the pan and fry for 4 minutes. Stir in the pancetta and wine.

4 Tie the thyme, bay leaf and parsley into a bundle and add to the pan. Bring to the boil, then simmer gently for 3–4 minutes. Pour over the guinea fowl and add seasoning. Cover and cook in the oven for 40 minutes.

5 Add the baby carrots and turnips to the casserole and cook, covered, for another 30 minutes, until the vegetables are just tender. Stir in the leeks and cook for a further 20 minutes, or until the vegetables are cooked.

6 Meanwhile, blanch the peas in boiling water for 2 minutes, then drain. Transfer the guinea fowl and vegetables to a warmed serving dish. Place the casserole on the hob and boil the juices vigorously over a high heat until they are reduced by about half.

7 Stir in the peas and cook gently for 2–3 minutes, then stir in the mustard and adjust the seasoning. Stir in most of the parsley and the mint. Pour this sauce over the guinea fowl or return the joints and vegetables to the casserole. Sprinkle the remaining parsley over the top and serve.

Per portion Energy 862kcal/3579kJ; Protein 52g; Carbohydrate 23.4g, of which sugars 11g; Fat 50.5g, of which saturates 13.6g; Cholesterol 227mg; Calcium 138mg; Fibre 8.3g; Sodium 558mg.

Rabbit salmorejo

Slow-cooked rabbit was a crucial part of the Spanish peasant diet, and this dish includes pounded garlic, bread and vinegar, giving it a classic Mediterranean character.

Serves 4

675g/1½lb rabbit, jointed

300ml/½ pint/1¼ cups dry white wine

15ml/1 tbsp sherry vinegar

several oregano sprigs

2 bay leaves

30ml/2 tbsp plain (all-purpose) flour

90ml/6 tbsp olive oil

175g/6oz baby (pearl) onions, peeled and left whole

4 garlic cloves, sliced

150ml/¼ pint/⅔ cup chicken stock

1 dried chilli, seeded and finely chopped

10ml/2 tsp paprika

salt and ground black pepper

fresh flat leaf parsley sprigs, to garnish (optional)

1 Put the rabbit in a bowl. Add the wine, vinegar, oregano and bay leaves and toss together. Marinate for several hours or overnight in the refrigerator.

2 Drain the rabbit, reserving the marinade, and pat it dry with kitchen paper. Season the flour and use to dust the marinated rabbit.

3 Heat the oil in a large, wide flameproof casserole or frying pan. Fry the rabbit pieces until golden on all sides, then remove them and set aside.

4 Fry the onions until they are beginning to colour, then reserve on a separate plate.

5 Add the garlic to the pan and fry, then add the strained marinade, with the chicken stock, chilli and paprika.

6 Return the rabbit and the reserved onions to the pan. Bring to a simmer, then cover and simmer gently for about 45 minutes until the rabbit is tender. Check the seasoning, adding more vinegar and paprika if necessary. Serve the dish garnished with a few sprigs of flat leaf parsley, if you like.

Cook's tip Rather than cooking on the stove, transfer the stew to an ovenproof dish and bake in the oven at 180°C/350°F/Gas 4 for about 50 minutes.

Per portion Energy 311kcal/1294kJ; Protein 23.2g; Carbohydrate 9.5g, of which sugars 2.6g; Fat 20.4g, of which saturates 4.1g; Cholesterol 83mg; Calcium 65mg; Fibre 0.9g; Sodium 52mg.

Meat dishes

Freshly baked pies, slow-cooked pot roasts
and flavoursome casseroles sum up all that
is best in country cooking. From simple
comfort food such as Sausage and Potato
Casserole to the classic Boeuf Bourguignon,
there is a meat dish for every occasion in this
chapter. Many of the recipes use economic
cuts of meat and seasonal vegetables,
so you can really make the most of the
revival in home cooking.

Pan-fried liver with bacon, sage and onions

Calf's liver would also be ideal for this recipe, but make sure not to overcook the liver or it will become tough. Serve with green leaves and a potato and root vegetable mash. You could also try adding mashed swede, parsnip or roast pumpkin to basic mashed potatoes.

Serves 4

450g/1lb lamb's liver

30ml/2 tbsp plain (all-purpose) flour

15ml/1 tbsp oil, plus extra if necessary

8 rindless streaky (fatty) bacon rashers (slices)

2 onions, thinly sliced

4 fresh sage leaves, finely chopped

150ml/½ pint/⅔ cup chicken or vegetable stock

salt and ground black pepper

Variations
• Other liver such as venison or ox could also be used in this recipe.
• A delicious addition would be a splash of Madeira or Marsala wine to add a sweet and sticky sauce – replace the stock with the wine and bubble down.

1 Pat the liver with kitchen paper, then trim it and cut on the diagonal to make thick strips. Season the flour and toss the liver in it until it is well coated, shaking off any excess flour.

2 Heat the oil in a large frying pan and add the bacon. Cook over medium heat until the fat runs out of the bacon and it is browned and crisp. Lift out and keep warm.

3 Add the onions and sage to the frying pan. Cook over medium heat for about 10–15 minutes, stirring occasionally, until the onions are soft and golden brown.

4 Carefully lift the onions out of the pan with a draining spoon and keep them warm.

5 Increase the heat and, adding extra oil if necessary, add the liver in a single layer. Cook for 4 minutes, turning once, until browned both sides.

6 Return the onions to the pan and pour in the stock. Bring to the boil and bubble gently for a minute or two, seasoning to taste. Serve topped with the bacon.

Per portion Energy 310kcal/1293kJ; Protein 28.7g; Carbohydrate 13.7g, of which sugars 5.7g; Fat 15.9g, of which saturates 4.4g; Cholesterol 500mg; Calcium 44mg; Fibre 1.6g; Sodium 400mg.

Pot-roast ham with mustard and cabbage

An updated version of traditional boiled bacon and cabbage, this recipe also takes its inspiration from the Italian country dish of pork cooked in milk. This technique helps to counteract the saltiness of the ham, and also keeps the meat deliciously moist.

Serves 4–6

1.3kg/3lb piece of gammon (smoked or cured ham) or boiling bacon

30ml/2 tbsp oil

2 large onions, sliced

1 bay leaf

750ml/1¼ pints/3 cups milk, plus extra if necessary

15ml/1 tbsp cornflour (cornstarch), dissolved in 15ml/1 tbsp milk

45ml/3 tbsp wholegrain mustard

15–30ml/2–3 tbsp single (light) cream (optional)

1 head of cabbage, such as Savoy, trimmed, ribs removed and leaves finely sliced

ground black pepper

1 Soak the bacon joint in cold water overnight. Heat 15ml/1 tbsp oil in a pan, add the onions and cook gently.

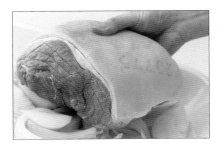

2 Place the joint on the bed of cooked onions. Add the bay leaf and milk, and season with pepper. Bring to the boil, cover and cook for about 1½ hours. Remove the meat from the pan and keep warm. Strain the cooking liquid. Reserve 300ml/½ pint/1¼ cups for the sauce and put the rest aside for soup.

3 Add the cornflour mixture to the reserved liquid and bring to the boil, stirring constantly. As it begins to thicken, stir in the wholegrain mustard and cream, if using.

4 Rinse the cabbage in cold running water and drain well.

5 Heat the remaining oil in a wok or large frying pan and stir-fry the cabbage for 2–3 minutes until cooked but still crunchy.

6 Slice the ham and serve on warmed serving plates with the mustard sauce and crisply cooked cabbage.

Per portion Energy 541kcal/2253kJ; Protein 58.4g; Carbohydrate 7.4g, of which sugars 5g; Fat 30.8g, of which saturates 9.4g; Cholesterol 77mg; Calcium 76mg; Fibre 2.1g; Sodium 2.87g.

Sausage and potato casserole

Be sure to use good meaty sausages for this traditional Irish recipe, slow cooking all the ingredients together to give the best results. Serve with some steamed buttered spinach.

Serves 4

15ml/1 tbsp vegetable oil

4 bacon rashers (strips), cut into 2.5cm/1in pieces

2 large onions, chopped

2 garlic cloves, crushed

8 large pork sausages

4 large baking potatoes, thinly sliced

1.5ml/¼ tsp fresh sage

300ml/½ pint/1¼ cups vegetable stock

salt and ground black pepper

soda bread, to serve

1 Preheat the oven to 180°C/350°F/ Gas 4. Grease a large ovenproof dish and set aside. Heat the oil in a frying pan. Add the bacon and fry for 2 minutes. Add the onions and fry for 5 minutes until golden. Add the garlic and fry for 1 minute, then remove the mixture from the pan and set aside. Then fry the sausages in the pan for 5 minutes until golden brown.

2 Arrange the potatoes in the base of the prepared dish. Spoon the bacon and onion mixture on top. Season with the salt and pepper and sprinkle with the fresh sage.

3 Pour on the stock and top with the sausages. Cover and bake for 1 hour. Serve hot with fresh soda bread.

Per portion Energy 553kcal/2305kJ; Protein 17.4g; Carbohydrate 48.7g, of which sugars 10g; Fat 33.4g, of which saturates 11.8g; Cholesterol 51mg; Calcium 74mg; Fibre 4g; Sodium 1019mg.

Mustard thatch lamb pie

This is a shepherd's pie with a twist. Adding mustard to the potato topping gives extra bite and a crunchy, golden topping. Serve with minted new peas or steamed broccoli.

Serves 4

800g/1¾lb floury potatoes, diced

60ml/4 tbsp milk

15ml/1 tbsp wholegrain
or French mustard

a little butter

450g/1lb lean lamb, minced (ground)

1 onion, chopped

2 celery sticks, thinly sliced

2 carrots, diced

30ml/2 tbsp cornflour blended into
150ml/¼ pint/⅔ cup lamb stock

15ml/1 tbsp Worcestershire sauce

30ml/2 tbsp chopped fresh rosemary,
or 10ml/2 tsp dried

salt and ground black pepper

fresh vegetables, to serve

1 Cook the potatoes in a large pan of boiling lightly salted water until tender. Drain well and mash until smooth, then stir in the milk, mustard, butter and seasoning to taste. Meanwhile, preheat the oven to 200°C/400°F/Gas 6.

2 Fry the lamb in a non-stick pan, breaking it up with a fork, until browned. Add the onion, celery and carrots and cook for 2–3 minutes, stirring, to stop the mixture sticking to the base.

3 Stir in the stock and cornflour mixture. Bring to the boil, stirring constantly, then remove from the heat. Stir in the Worcestershire sauce and rosemary and season with salt and pepper to taste.

4 Turn the lamb mixture into a 1.75 litre/3 pint/7 cup ovenproof dish and spread over the potato topping evenly, swirling with the edge of a palette knife. Bake for 30–35 minutes until golden on the top. Serve hot with a selection of fresh vegetables.

Variations
• The original shepherd's pie is made with lamb. It can be made with minced beef, in which case it is a cottage pie.
• To vary the potato topping, try adding horseradish – either creamed or, for an even stronger flavour, freshly grated.

Per portion Energy 371kcal/1561kJ; Protein 26.5g; Carbohydrate 37.9g, of which sugars 7.7g; Fat 13.7g, of which saturates 6.2g; Cholesterol 86mg; Calcium 68mg; Fibre 3.3g; Sodium 194mg.

Lamb stew with shallots and new potatoes

Italian gremolata made with lemon rind, garlic and parsley is a piquant garnish
for the lamb. Traditionally served with osso buco, it is also good served with fish.

Serves 6

1kg/2¼lb boneless shoulder of lamb, trimmed of fat and cut into 5cm/2in cubes

1 garlic clove, finely chopped

finely grated rind of ½ lemon and juice of 1 lemon

90ml/6 tbsp olive oil

45ml/3 tbsp plain (all-purpose) flour

1 large onion, sliced

5 anchovy fillets in olive oil, drained

2.5ml/½ tsp caster (superfine) sugar

300ml/½ pint/1¼ cups white wine

475ml/16fl oz/2 cups lamb stock or half stock and half water

1 fresh bay leaf

fresh thyme sprig

fresh parsley sprig

500g/1¼lb small new potatoes

250g/9oz shallots, peeled but left whole

45ml/3 tbsp double (heavy) cream (optional)

salt and ground black pepper

For the gremolata

1 garlic clove, finely chopped

finely shredded rind of ½ lemon

45ml/3 tbsp chopped fresh flat leaf parsley

1 Mix the lamb with the garlic and the rind and juice of ½ lemon. Season with pepper and mix in 15ml/1 tbsp olive oil, then leave to marinate for 12–24 hours.

2 Drain the lamb, reserving the marinade, and pat the lamb dry with kitchen paper. Preheat the oven to 180°C/350°F/Gas 4.

3 Heat 30ml/2 tbsp olive oil in a large, heavy frying pan. Season the flour with salt and pepper and toss the lamb in it to coat, shaking off any excess. Seal the lamb on all sides in the hot oil. Do this in batches, transferring each batch of lamb to an ovenproof pan or flameproof casserole as you brown it. You may need to add an extra 15ml/1 tbsp olive oil to the pan.

4 Reduce the heat, add another 15ml/1 tbsp oil to the pan and cook the onion gently over a very low heat, stirring frequently, for 10 minutes, until softened and golden but not browned.

5 Add the anchovies and caster sugar, and cook, mashing the anchovies into the soft onion with a wooden spoon until well combined.

6 Add the reserved marinade, increase the heat a little and cook for about 1–2 minutes, then pour in the wine and stock or stock and water and bring to the boil. Simmer gently for about 5 minutes, then pour over the lamb.

7 Tie the bay leaf, thyme and parsley together and add to the lamb. Season with salt and pepper, then cover tightly and cook in the oven for 1 hour. Stir the potatoes into the stew and cook for a further 20 minutes.

8 Meanwhile, to make the gremolata, chop all the ingredients together finely. Place in a dish, cover and set aside.

9 Heat the remaining oil in a frying pan and brown the shallots on all sides, then stir them into the lamb.

10 Cover and cook for a further 30–40 minutes, until the lamb is tender. Transfer the lamb and vegetables to a dish and keep warm. Discard the herbs.

11 Boil the cooking juices to reduce and concentrate them, then add the cream, if using, and simmer for 2–3 minutes.

12 Adjust the seasoning, adding a little lemon juice to taste. Pour this sauce over the lamb, sprinkle the gremolata on top and serve immediately.

Per portion Energy 553kcal/2311kJ; Protein 37g; Carbohydrate 26.2g, of which sugars 5.3g; Fat 30.6g, of which saturates 10.4g; Cholesterol 128mg; Calcium 79mg; Fibre 2.7g; Sodium 261mg.

Roast shoulder of lamb with garlic potatoes

The potatoes are basted in the lamb juices while cooking, and become wonderfully garlicky, fragrant and sticky. Return the potatoes to the oven to keep warm while you leave the lamb to rest before carving, then serve along with a selection of seasonal vegetables.

Serves 4–6

675g/1½lb waxy potatoes, peeled and cut into large dice

12 garlic cloves, unpeeled

1 whole shoulder of lamb

45ml/3 tbsp olive oil

salt and ground black pepper

Cook's tip Shoulder of lamb is naturally sweet as it has fat distributed within the meat. When buying the lamb, make sure it still has the bone as this will add to the flavour when it is cooking.

1 Preheat the oven to 180°C/350°F/ Gas 4. Put the potatoes and garlic cloves into a large roasting pan and season with salt and pepper. Pour over 30ml/2 tbsp of the oil and toss the potatoes and garlic to coat.

2 Place a rack over the roasting pan, so that it is not touching the potatoes. Place the lamb on the rack and drizzle over the remaining oil. Season with salt and pepper.

3 Roast the lamb and potatoes for about 2–2½ hours, or until the lamb is cooked through.

4 Halfway through the cooking time, carefully take the lamb and the rack off the roasting pan and turn the potatoes to ensure even cooking. Transfer the lamb, potatoes and garlic to a warmed serving platter.

Per portion Energy 668kcal/2775kJ; Protein 29.2g; Carbohydrate 20.8g, of which sugars 1.7g; Fat 52.6g, of which saturates 24.1g; Cholesterol 113mg; Calcium 22mg; Fibre 1.8g; Sodium 123mg.

Veal and ham pie

Historically, the English love pies made with mutton and pork. This splendid version contains diced veal, gammon and hard-boiled eggs. The flavours of the two meats marry perfectly in the delicate filling. Serve with green cabbage leaves and buttery mashed potato.

Serves 4

450g/1lb boneless shoulder of veal, diced

225g/8oz lean gammon (smoked or cured ham), diced

15ml/1 tbsp plain (all-purpose) flour

large pinch each of dry mustard and ground black pepper

25g/1oz/2 tbsp butter

15ml/1 tbsp sunflower oil

1 onion, chopped

600ml/1 pint/2½ cups chicken or veal stock

2 eggs, hard-boiled and sliced

30ml/2 tbsp chopped fresh parsley

For the pastry

175g/6oz/1½ cups plain (all-purpose) flour

75g/3oz/6 tbsp butter

iced water, to mix

beaten egg, to glaze

1 Preheat the oven to 180°C/350°F/ Gas 4. Mix the veal and gammon in a bowl. Season the flour with the mustard and pepper, then add it to the meat and toss well. Heat the butter and oil in a casserole until sizzling, then cook the meat mixture in batches until golden on all sides. Remove the meat from the pan.

2 Cook the onion in the fat remaining in the casserole until softened, but not coloured. Gradually stir in the stock, then replace the meat mixture and stir. Cover and cook in the oven for 1½ hours, or until the veal is tender.

3 To make the pastry, sift the flour into a bowl and rub in the butter with your fingers. Mix in enough iced water to bind the mixture into clumps, then press these together with your fingertips to make a dough.

4 Spoon the cooked veal and gammon mixture into a 1.5 litre/2½ pint/6¼ cup pie dish. Arrange the slices of hard-boiled egg over the top and sprinkle with the chopped parsley.

5 Roll out the pastry on a lightly floured work surface to about 4cm/1½in larger than the top of the pie dish.

6 Cover the pie dish with the pastry lid. Press the pastry around the rim to seal in the filling and cut off any excess. Use the blunt edge of a knife to tap the outside edge of the pastry, pressing it down with your finger as you seal in the filling. Pinch the pastry between your fingers to flute the edge.

7 Roll out any remaining pastry and cut out decorative shapes to garnish the top of the pie. Brush with beaten egg and bake for 30–40 minutes, or until the pastry is well-risen and golden brown. Serve hot with steamed green cabbage and creamy mashed potato.

Per portion Energy 621kcal/2595kJ; Protein 42.4g; Carbohydrate 39.2g, of which sugars 2.6g; Fat 33.8g, of which saturates 17.2g; Cholesterol 281mg; Calcium 128mg; Fibre 2.3g; Sodium 1007mg.

Pot roast beef with stout

Use a boned and rolled joint such as brisket, silverside or topside for this slow-cooked dish, where the vegetables are cooked with the beef and the meat becomes meltingly tender.

Serves 6

30ml/2 tbsp vegetable oil

900g/2lb rolled brisket of beef

2 medium onions, roughly chopped

2 celery sticks, thickly sliced

450g/1lb carrots, cut into large chunks

675g/1½lb potatoes, peeled and cut into large chunks

30ml/2 tbsp plain (all-purpose) flour

450ml/¾ pint/ 2 cups beef stock

300ml/½ pint/1¼ cups stout

1 bay leaf

45ml/3 tbsp chopped fresh thyme

5ml/1 tsp soft light brown sugar

30ml/2 tbsp wholegrain mustard

15ml/1 tbsp tomato purée (paste)

salt and ground black pepper

1 Preheat the oven to 180°C/350°F/ Gas 4. Heat the oil in a large flameproof casserole and brown the beef until golden brown all over.

2 Lift the beef from the pan and drain on kitchen paper. Add the onions to the pan and cook for about 4 minutes, until just beginning to soften and brown.

3 Add the celery, carrots and potatoes to the casserole and cook over a medium heat for 2–3 minutes, or until they are just beginning to colour.

4 Add the flour and cook for a further 1 minute, stirring constantly. Gradually pour in the beef stock and the stout. Heat until the mixture comes to the boil, stirring frequently.

5 Stir in the bay leaf, thyme, sugar, mustard, tomato purée and seasoning. Place the meat on top, cover tightly and transfer the casserole to the hot oven.

6 Cook for about 2½ hours, or until tender. Adjust the seasoning, to taste. To serve, carve the beef into thick slices and serve with the vegetables and plenty of gravy.

Per portion Energy 415kcal/1743kJ; Protein 36g; Carbohydrate 35.6g, of which sugars 13.1g; Fat 14g, of which saturates 4.4g; Cholesterol 81mg; Calcium 66mg; Fibre 4.2g; Sodium 284mg.

Braised beef and country vegetables

A dish which, in the past, would have been gently left to cook all day, this casserole is just as impressive slow cooked for a few hours. It is delicious with suet dumplings or crusty bread.

Serves 4–6

1kg/2¼lb lean stewing steak, cut into 5cm/2in cubes

45ml/3 tbsp plain (all-purpose) flour

45ml/3 tbsp oil

1 large onion, thinly sliced

1 large carrot, thickly sliced

2 celery sticks, finely chopped

300ml/½ pint/¼ cup beef stock

30ml/2 tbsp tomato purée (paste)

5ml/1 tsp dried mixed herbs

15ml/1 tbsp dark muscovado (molasses) sugar

225g/8oz baby potatoes, halved

2 leeks, thinly sliced

salt and ground black pepper

Variation Replace the potatoes with dumplings. Sift 175g/6oz/1½ cups self-raising (self-rising) flour and stir in 75g/3oz/½ cup shredded suet (US chilled, grated shortening), 30ml/2 tbsp chopped parsley and seasoning. Stir in water to make a soft dough and divide the mixture into 12 balls. In step 6, stir in the leeks and put the dumplings on top. Cover and cook for 15–20 minutes more.

1 Preheat the oven to 150°C/300°F/ Gas 2. Season the flour and use to coat the beef cubes.

2 Heat the oil in a large, flameproof casserole. Add a small batch of meat, cook quickly until browned on all sides and, with a slotted spoon, lift out. Repeat with the remaining beef.

3 Add the onion, carrot and celery to the casserole. Cook over medium heat for about 10 minutes, stirring frequently, until they begin to soften and brown slightly on the edges.

4 Return the meat to the casserole and add the stock, tomato purée, herbs and sugar, at the same time scraping up any sediment that has stuck to the casserole. Heat until the liquid nearly comes to the boil.

5 Cover with a tight fitting lid and put into the hot oven. Cook for 2–2½ hours, or until the beef is tender.

6 Gently stir in the potatoes and leeks, cover and continue cooking for a further 30 minutes or until the potatoes are soft.

Per portion Energy 450kcal/1880kJ; Protein 41.3g; Carbohydrate 23.6g, of which sugars 10.3g; Fat 21.7g, of which saturates 7.3g; Cholesterol 97mg; Calcium 63mg; Fibre 3.5g; Sodium 137mg.

Boeuf Bourguignon

Beef cooked 'Burgundy style' in red wine with chopped bacon, baby onions and mushrooms and simmered for hours at a low temperature produces a rich, dark gravy and melt-in-the-mouth meat. Serve with creamy mashed potato and croûtons of bread fried in duck fat.

Serves 6

175g/6oz rindless streaky (fatty) bacon rashers (strips), chopped

900g/2lb lean braising steak, such as top rump of beef or braising steak

30ml/2 tbsp plain (all-purpose) flour

45ml/3 tbsp sunflower oil

25g/1oz/2 tbsp butter

12 shallots

2 garlic cloves, crushed

175g/6oz/2½ cups mushrooms, sliced

450ml/¾ pint/scant 2 cups robust red wine

150ml/¼ pint/⅔ cup beef stock or consommé

1 bay leaf

2 sprigs each of fresh thyme, parsley and marjoram

salt and ground black pepper

Variation Instead of the rindless streaky (fatty) bacon rashers (strips), use lardons, which are available from supermarkets.

1 Preheat the oven to 160°C/325°F/Gas 3. Heat a large flameproof casserole, then add the bacon and cook, stirring occasionally, until the pieces are crisp and golden brown.

2 Meanwhile, cut the meat into 2.5cm/1in cubes. Season the flour and use to coat the meat. Use a draining spoon to remove the bacon from the casserole and set aside. Add and heat the oil, then brown the beef in batches and set aside with the bacon.

3 Add the butter to the fat remaining in the casserole. Cook the shallots and crushed garlic until just starting to colour, then add the sliced mushrooms and cook for a further 5 minutes. Replace the bacon and meat, and stir in the wine and stock or consommé. Tie the bay leaf, thyme, parsley and marjoram together into a bouquet garni and add to the casserole.

4 Cover and cook in the oven for 1½ hours, or until the meat is tender, stirring once or twice. Season to taste and serve the casserole with creamy mashed root vegetables, such as celeriac and potatoes.

Cook's tip Boeuf Bourguignon freezes very well. Transfer the mixture to a dish so that it cools quickly, then pour it into a rigid plastic container. Push all the cubes of meat down into the sauce or they will dry out. Freeze for up to 2 months. Thaw overnight in the refrigerator, then transfer to a flameproof casserole and add 150ml/¼ pint/⅔ cup water. Stir well, bring to the boil, stirring occasionally, and simmer steadily for at least 10 minutes, or until the meat is piping hot.

Per portion Energy 749kcal/3117kJ; Protein 63.3g; Carbohydrate 15.2g, of which sugars 8.8g; Fat 40.3g, of which saturates 14g; Cholesterol 167mg; Calcium 69mg; Fibre 2.8g; Sodium 868mg.

Braised oxtail

While oxtail requires long, slow cooking to tenderize the meat, the resulting complex, dark flavours are well worth the effort. This dish is traditionally served with plain boiled potatoes to soak up the rich gravy, though mashed potatoes would be good too.

Serves 6

2 oxtails, trimmed, cut into pieces, total weight about 1.5kg/3lb 6oz

30ml/2 tbsp flour seasoned with salt and pepper

45ml/3 tbsp oil

2 large onions, sliced

2 celery sticks, sliced

4 medium carrots, sliced

1 litre/1¾ pints/4 cups beef stock

15ml/1 tbsp tomato purée (paste)

finely grated rind of 1 small orange

2 bay leaves

few sprigs of fresh thyme

salt and ground black pepper

chopped fresh parsley, to garnish

1 Preheat the oven to 150°C/300°F/Gas 2. Coat the pieces of oxtail in the seasoned flour, shaking off and reserving any excess.

2 Heat 30ml/2 tbsp oil in a large flameproof casserole and add the oxtail in batches, cooking quickly until browned all over. Lift out and set aside. Add the remaining oil to the pan, and stir in the onions, celery and carrots.

3 Cook the vegetables quickly, stirring occasionally, until beginning to brown. Tip in any reserved flour, then add the stock, tomato purée and orange rind.

Cook's tip This dish benefits from being made in advance. When cooled completely, any fat can be removed before reheating.

4 Heat until bubbles begin to rise to the surface, then add the herbs, cover and put into the hot oven. Cook for 3½–4 hours until the oxtail is very tender.

5 Remove from the oven and leave to stand, covered, for 10 minutes before skimming off the surface fat. Adjust the seasoning and garnish with parsley.

Per portion Energy 341kcal/1426kJ; Protein 30.9g; Carbohydrate 13.6g, of which sugars 7.7g; Fat 18.6g, of which saturates 0.7g; Cholesterol 0mg; Calcium 54mg; Fibre 2.3g; Sodium 203mg.

Steak, mushroom and ale pie

This dish is a firm favourite on menus at restaurants specializing in traditional country fare. Preparing the filling the day before and allowing the meat and vegetables to rest overnight ensures a particularly tasty filling. The pie can be ready relatively quickly simply by topping with the pastry and baking. Serve with seasonal vegetables or a side salad.

Serves 4

25g/1oz/2 tbsp butter

1 large onion, finely chopped

115g/4oz/1½ cups chestnut or button (white) mushrooms, halved

900g/2lb lean beef in one piece, such as rump or braising steak

30ml/2 tbsp plain (all-purpose) flour

45ml/3 tbsp sunflower oil

300ml/½ pint/1¼ cups stout or brown ale

300ml/½ pint/1¼ cups beef stock or consommé

500g/1¼lb puff pastry, thawed if frozen

beaten egg, to glaze

salt and ground black pepper

1 Melt the butter in a large, flameproof casserole, add the onion and cook gently, stirring occasionally, for about 5 minutes, or until it is softened. Add the halved mushrooms and continue cooking for a further 5 minutes, stirring.

2 Meanwhile, trim the meat and cut it into 2.5cm/1in cubes. Season the flour and toss the meat in it.

3 Remove the onion mixture from the casserole and set aside. Add the oil, then brown the steak in batches.

4 Replace the vegetables, then stir in the stout or ale and stock or consommé. Bring to the boil, reduce the heat and simmer for 1 hour, stirring occasionally. Season to taste and transfer to a 1.5 litre/2½ pint/6½ cup pie dish. Cover and leave to cool. If possible, chill the meat filling overnight, as this allows the flavour to develop. Preheat the oven to 230°C/450°F/Gas 8.

5 Roll out the pastry in the shape of the dish and about 4cm/1½in larger all around. Cut a 2.5cm/1in strip from the edge of the pastry. Brush the rim of the dish with water and press the pastry strip on it. Brush the pastry rim with beaten egg and cover the pie with the pastry lid. Press the lid firmly in place, then trim of the excess.

6 Use the blunt edge of a knife to tap the outside edge of the pastry, pressing it down with your finger as you seal in the filling. (This technique is known as knocking up.)

7 Pinch the pastry between your fingers to flute the edge. Roll out any remaining pastry trimmings and cut out shapes to garnish the pie, brushing the shapes with a little beaten egg before pressing them lightly in place.

8 Make a hole in the middle of the pie to allow steam to escape, brush the top carefully with beaten egg and chill for 10 minutes to rest the pastry.

9 Bake the pie for 15 minutes, then reduce the oven temperature to 200°C/400°F/Gas 6 and bake for a further 15–20 minutes, or until the pastry is risen and golden. Let the pie rest for a minute or two before serving.

Per portion Energy 1061kcal/4423kJ; Protein 58.8g; Carbohydrate 59.3g, of which sugars 7.6g; Fat 65.3g, of which saturates 24g; Cholesterol 164mg; Calcium 129mg; Fibre 3.2g; Sodium 622mg.

Puddings and desserts

The aroma of a warm, golden pumpkin pie is a delectable part of autumn country cooking, while the abundant fruits of summer make luscious pastry dishes. The puddings and desserts in this chapter offer something for every sweet tooth. There are few simpler recipes than those for rhubarb fools – they are easy to make and look very impressive.

Classic treacle tart

A way of using up stale breadcrumbs, this tart is actually based on golden syrup rather than treacle or molasses. There many variations on the basic recipe, but the hint of lemon in this one makes it particularly good. Serve it warm or cold, with custard or cream.

3 Mix the breadcrumbs with the ginger, if using, and spread the mixture over the bottom of the pastry. Gently warm the syrup with the lemon rind and juice (on the stove or in the microwave) until quite runny and pour evenly over the breadcrumbs.

4 Gather the reserved pastry trimmings into a ball, roll out on a lightly floured surface and cut into long, narrow strips. Twist these into spirals and arrange them in a lattice pattern on top of the tart, pressing them on to the edge to secure. Trim the ends.

5 Put into the hot oven and cook for about 25 minutes until the pastry is golden brown and cooked through and the filling has set.

Serves 6

175g/6oz/1½ cups plain (all-purpose) flour

pinch of salt

40g/1½oz/3 tbsp lard

40g/1½oz/3 tbsp butter, diced

75g/3oz/1½ cups fresh breadcrumbs

2.5ml/½ tsp ground ginger (optional)

225g/8oz/1 cup golden (light corn) syrup

grated rind and juice of 1 lemon

1 Sift the flour and salt into a bowl and add the lard and butter. With the fingertips, rub the fats into the flour until the mixture resembles fine breadcrumbs. Stir in about 45ml/3 tbsp cold water until the mixture can be gathered together into a smooth ball of dough. Wrap the pastry and refrigerate for 30 minutes. Meanwhile, preheat the oven to 190°C/375°F/Gas 5.

2 Roll out the pastry on a lightly floured surface and use to line a 20cm/8in flan tin (pan) or pie plate, reserving the trimmings.

Variations
• You could omit the lemon rind and juice.
• Sometimes finely crushed cornflakes are used in place of the breadcrumbs.

Per portion Energy 420kcal/1764kJ; Protein 4.1g; Carbohydrate 63.5g, of which sugars 35.1g; Fat 18.4g, of which saturates 11.3g; Cholesterol 46mg; Calcium 62mg; Fibre 1.1g; Sodium 344mg.

Bakewell tart

This is a modern version of the Bakewell pudding, which is made with puff pastry and has a custard-like almond filling. It is said to be the result of a 19th-century kitchen accident and is still baked in the original shop in Bakewell, England. Serve with a hot cup of tea.

Serves 4

For the pastry

115g/4oz/1 cup plain
(all-purpose) flour

pinch of salt

50g/2oz/4 tbsp butter, diced

For the filling

30ml/2 tbsp raspberry or
apricot jam

2 whole eggs and 2 extra yolks

115g/4oz/generous ½ cup caster
(superfine) sugar

115g/4oz/½ cup butter, melted

55g/2oz/⅔ cup ground almonds

few drops of almond extract

icing (confectioners') sugar, to dust

1 Sift the flour and salt and rub in the butter until the mixture resembles fine crumbs. Stir in about 30ml/2 tbsp cold water and gather into a smooth ball of dough. Wrap and chill for 30 minutes. Preheat the oven to 200°C/400°F/Gas 6.

2 Roll out the pastry and use to line an 18cm/7in loose-based flan tin (pan). Spread the jam over the pastry.

3 Whisk the eggs, egg yolks and sugar together in a large bowl until the mixture is thick and pale. Gently stir in the melted butter, ground almonds and almond extract. Mix well together to combine.

4 Pour the mixture over the jam in the pastry case (pie shell). Put the tart into the hot oven and cook for 30 minutes until just set and browned. Sift a little icing sugar over the top before serving warm or at room temperature.

Per portion Energy 700kcal/2919kJ; Protein 10.8g; Carbohydrate 57.1g, of which sugars 36.7g; Fat 49.9g, of which saturates 17.1g; Cholesterol 257mg; Calcium 110mg; Fibre 0.9g; Sodium 394mg.

Peach and blueberry pie

With its attractive lattice pastry top, this colourful pie is bursting with plump blueberries and juicy peaches. It is good hot, or can be wrapped in its tin and transported to a picnic.

Serves 8

225g/8oz/2 cups plain (all-purpose) flour

2.5ml/½ tsp salt

5ml/1 tsp granulated (white) sugar

150g/5oz/10 tbsp cold butter or margarine, diced

1 egg yolk

30–45ml/2–3 tbsp iced water

30ml/2 tbsp milk, for glazing

For the filling

6 peaches, peeled, pitted and sliced

225g/8oz/2 cups fresh blueberries

150g/5oz/¾ cup granulated sugar

30ml/2 tbsp fresh lemon juice

40g/1½oz/⅓ cup plain (all-purpose) flour

pinch of grated nutmeg

25g/1oz/2 tbsp butter or margarine, cut into pea-size pieces

1 For the pastry, sift the flour, salt and sugar into a bowl. Rub the butter or margarine into the dry ingredients as quickly as possible until the mixture is crumbly and resembles breadcrumbs.

2 Mix the egg yolk with 30ml/2 tbsp of the iced water and sprinkle over the flour mixture. Combine with a fork until the pastry holds together. If the pastry is too crumbly, add a little more water, 5ml/1 tsp at a time. Gather the pastry into a ball and flatten into a disk. Wrap in clear film (plastic wrap) and chill for at least 20 minutes.

3 Roll out two-thirds of the pastry between two sheets of baking parchment to a thickness of about 3mm/⅛in. Use to line a 23cm/9in fluted tin (pan). Trim all around, leaving a 1cm/½in overhang, then trim the edges with a sharp knife.

4 Gather the trimmings and remaining pastry into a ball, and roll out to a thickness of about 6mm/¼in. Using a pastry wheel or sharp knife, cut strips 1cm/½in wide. Chill the pastry case and the strips for 20 minutes. Preheat the oven to 200°C/400°F/ Gas 6.

5 Line the pastry case with baking parchment and fill with dried beans. Bake until the pastry case is just set, 12–15 minutes. Remove from the oven and carefully lift out the paper with the beans. Prick the bottom of the pastry case all over with a fork, then return to the oven and bake for 5 minutes more. Let the pastry case cool slightly before filling. Leave the oven on.

6 In a mixing bowl, combine the peach slices with the blueberries, sugar, lemon juice, flour and nutmeg. Spoon the fruit mixture evenly into the pastry case. Dot with the pieces of butter or margarine.

7 Weave a lattice top with the chilled pastry strips, pressing the ends to the baked pastry-case edge. Brush the strips with the milk.

8 Bake the pie for 15 minutes. Reduce the heat to 180°C/350°F/Gas 4, and continue baking until the filling is tender and bubbling and the pastry lattice is golden, about 30 minutes more. If the pastry gets too brown, cover loosely with a piece of foil. Serve the pie warm or at room temperature.

Cook's tip To peel stone (pit) fruits, place them in a large heat-proof bowl and cover with boiling water. Leave for 2–3 minutes until the skins wrinkle, then drain. The skin should slide off easily.

Per portion Energy 391kcal/1640kJ; Protein 4.7g; Carbohydrate 53g, of which sugars 27.7g; Fat 19.3g, of which saturates 11.7g; Cholesterol 72mg; Calcium 86mg; Fibre 2.9g; Sodium 139mg.

Pecan pie

Almost an American institution, this classic country pie has a golden crust with a dense maple syrup filling topped with pecans halves. Serve warm with whipped cream.

Serves 8

3 eggs

pinch of salt

200g/7oz/scant 1 cup soft dark brown sugar

120ml/4fl oz/½ cup golden (light corn) syrup

30ml/2 tbsp fresh lemon juice

75g/3oz/6 tbsp butter, melted

150g/5oz/1¼ cups chopped pecan nuts

50g/2oz/½ cup pecan halves

For the pastry

175g/6oz/1½ cups plain (all-purpose) flour

15ml/1 tbsp caster (superfine) sugar

5ml/1 tsp baking powder

2.5ml/½ tsp salt

75g/3oz/6 tbsp cold unsalted (sweet) butter, cut in pieces

1 egg yolk

45–60ml/3–4 tbsp whipping cream

1 For the pastry, sift the flour, sugar, baking powder and salt into a bowl. Add the butter and cut in with a pastry blender until the mixture resembles coarse breadcrumbs.

2 In a bowl, beat together the egg yolk and cream until blended. Pour the mixture into the flour mixture and stir with a fork.

3 Gather the pastry into a ball. On a lightly floured surface, roll out 3mm/⅛in thick and transfer to a 23cm/9in fluted tin (pan).

4 Trim the overhang and flute the edge with your fingers. Chill for at least 20 minutes.

5 Preheat a baking sheet in the middle of a 200°C/400°F/Gas 6 oven. In a bowl, lightly whisk the eggs and salt. Add the sugar, syrup, lemon juice and butter. Mix well and stir in the chopped nuts.

6 Pour into the pastry case (pie shell) and arrange the pecan halves in concentric circles on top. Bake for 10 minutes. Reduce the heat to 170°C/325°F/Gas 3 and continue baking for 25 minutes.

Per portion Energy 587kcal/2449kJ; Protein 7.5g; Carbohydrate 56.7g, of which sugars 39.6g; Fat 38.3g, of which saturates 13.4g; Cholesterol 142mg; Calcium 82mg; Fibre 1.9g; Sodium 185mg.

Thanksgiving pumpkin pie

A version of this dish was baked by the earliest American settlers, and Thanksgiving would not be complete without it. Using canned pumpkin makes it a very easy pie to make.

Serves 8

450g/1lb cooked or canned pumpkin

250ml/8fl oz/1 cup whipping cream

2 eggs

115g/4oz/½ cup soft dark brown sugar

60ml/4 tbsp golden (light corn) syrup

7.5ml/1½ tsp ground cinnamon

5ml/1 tsp ground ginger

1.5ml/¼ tsp ground cloves

2.5ml/½ tsp salt

For the pastry

175g/6oz/1½ cups plain (all-purpose) flour

2.5ml/½ tsp salt

75g/3oz/6 tbsp cold butter, cut into pieces

40g/1½oz/3 tbsp cold white vegetable fat (shortening), cut into pieces

45–60ml/3–4 tbsp iced water

1 egg, beaten

1 For the pastry, sift the flour and salt into a bowl. Cut in the butter and fat until it resembles coarse crumbs. Bind with iced water. Wrap in clear film (plastic wrap) and chill for 20 minutes.

2 Roll out the dough and line a 23cm/9in fluted pie tin (pan). Trim off the overhang. Roll out the trimmings and cut out leaf shapes.

3 Chill for about 20 minutes. Preheat the oven to 200°C/400°F/Gas 6.

4 Line the pastry case with baking parchment. Fill with baking beans and bake for 12 minutes. Remove paper and beans and bake until golden, 6–8 minutes more. Reduce the heat to 190°C/375°F/Gas 5.

5 Beat together the pumpkin, cream, eggs, sugar, golden syrup, spices and salt. Pour into the pastry case and bake for 25 minutes. Brush the pastry leaves with egg and place around the top of the pie. Bake for 10–15 minutes more.

Per portion Energy 434kcal/1809kJ; Protein 6.2g; Carbohydrate 35.3g, of which sugars 19.4g; Fat 30.8g, of which saturates 13.8g; Cholesterol 94mg; Calcium 108mg; Fibre 1.2g; Sodium 60mg.

Rhubarb fool

This is a quick and simple dessert that makes the most of rhubarb when it is in season. You can use early or 'forced' rhubarb, which is a ravishing pink and needs very little cooking. Try adding a few drops of rosewater to the fruit as it cooks, and serve with shortbread.

1 Cut the rhubarb into pieces and wash thoroughly. Stew over a low heat with just the water clinging to it and the sugar. This takes about 10 minutes. Set aside to cool.

2 Pass the rhubarb through a fine sieve (strainer) so you have a thick purée.

Serves 4

450g/1lb rhubarb, trimmed

75g/3oz/scant ½ cup soft light brown sugar

whipped double (heavy) cream and ready-made thick custard (see step 3)

Variations
• You can use another fruit if you like for this dessert – try bramble fruits or apples. Other stewed fruits also work well, such as prunes or peaches. For something a little more exotic, you could try mangoes.
• For a low-fat option, substitute natural (plain) yogurt for the cream.

3 Use equal parts of the purée, the whipped double cream and ready-made thick custard. Combine the purée and custard first, then fold in the cream. Chill in the refrigerator before serving. Serve with heather honey.

Per portion Energy 439kcal/1828kJ; Protein 4.6g; Carbohydrate 34.1g, of which sugars 31.8g; Fat 31.7g, of which saturates 18.9g; Cholesterol 80mg; Calcium 233mg; Fibre 1.6g; Sodium 74mg.

Poached spiced pears

The fragrant aroma of pears is greatly enhanced by gently poaching them in either spiced liquor or wine. Serve this dish warm or cold, with some cream whipped with icing sugar and Poire William, and perhaps some crisp, sweet biscuits to give a contrasting texture.

Serves 4

115g/4oz/½ cup caster (superfine) sugar

grated rind and juice of 1 lemon

2.5ml/½ tsp ground ginger

1 small cinnamon stick

2 whole cloves

4 firm ripe pears

Variations
• Omit the spices and instead flavour the water with ginger or elderflower cordial.
• Use white wine in place of water.

1 Put the sugar in a pan with 300ml/½ pint/1½ cups water, the lemon rind and juice, ginger and spices. Heat, stirring, until the sugar has dissolved.

2 Peel the pears, cut them in half lengthways and remove their cores.

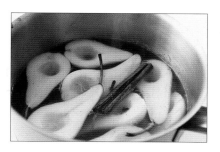

3 Add the pear halves to the pan and bring just to the boil. Cover and simmer gently for about 5 minutes or until the pears are tender, turning them over in the syrup occasionally during cooking. Remove from the heat and leave to cool in the syrup before serving.

Per portion Energy 93kcal/392kJ; Protein 0.5g; Carbohydrate 23.6g, of which sugars 23.6g; Fat 0.2g, of which saturates 0g; Cholesterol 0mg; Calcium 17mg; Fibre 3.3g; Sodium 6mg.

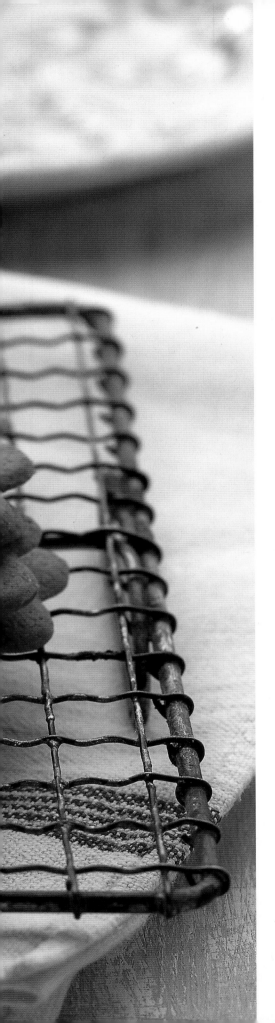

Bread, biscuits and bakes

A country meal is not complete without a piece of bread, and there are few more welcoming aromas than a home-baked loaf. For those with a sweet tooth, this chapter also includes recipes for tempting shortbreads, biscuits, cakes and muffins – all essential country teatime treats.

Poppyseed bloomer

This satisfying white poppyseed bread, which is a version of the chunky baton loaf found throughout Europe, is made using a slower rising method and with less yeast than usual. It produces a longer-keeping loaf with a fuller flavour. The dough takes about 8 hours to rise, so you'll need to start making the bread early in the morning.

Makes 1 large loaf

675g/1½ lb/6 cups unbleached white bread flour

10ml/2 tsp salt

15g/½ oz fresh yeast

430ml/15fl oz/1⅞ cups water

For the topping

2.5ml/½ tsp salt

30ml/2 tbsp water

poppy seeds, for sprinkling

Cook's tip You can get the cracked appearance of this loaf by spraying the oven with water before baking. If the underside is not crusty at the end, turn the loaf over, switch off the heat and leave in the oven for 5–10 minutes.

1 Lightly grease a baking sheet. Sift the flour and salt together into a large bowl and make a well in the centre.

2 Mix the yeast and 150ml/¼ pint/⅔ cup of the water in a bowl. Mix in the remaining water. Add to the centre of the flour. Mix, gradually incorporating the surrounding flour, until the mixture forms a firm dough.

3 Turn out on to a lightly floured surface and knead the dough for at least 10 minutes, until smooth and elastic. Place the dough in a lightly oiled bowl, cover with lightly oiled clear film (plastic wrap) and leave to rise, at cool room temperature, about 15–18°C/60–65°F, for 5–6 hours, or until doubled in bulk.

4 Knock back (punch down) the dough, turn out on to a lightly floured surface and knead it thoroughly and quite hard for about 5 minutes. Return the dough to the bowl, and re-cover. Leave to rise, at cool room temperature, for 2 hours.

5 Knock back again and repeat the thorough kneading. Leave the dough to rest for 5 minutes, then roll out on a lightly floured surface into a rectangle 2.5cm/1in thick. Roll the dough up from one long side and shape it into a square-ended thick baton shape about 33 × 13cm/13 × 5in.

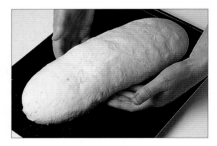

6 Place it seam side up on a lightly floured baking sheet, cover and leave to rest for 15 minutes. Turn the loaf over and place on the greased baking sheet. Plump up by tucking the dough under the sides and ends. Using a sharp knife, cut six diagonal slashes on the top.

7 Leave to rest, covered, in a warm place, for 10 minutes. Meanwhile preheat the oven to 230°C/450°F/Gas 8.

8 Mix the salt and water together and brush this glaze over the bread. Sprinkle with poppy seeds. Spray the oven with water, bake the bread immediately for 20 minutes, then reduce the oven temperature to 200°C/400°F/Gas 6. Bake for 25 minutes more, or until golden. Transfer to a wire rack to cool.

Variation You could also use sesame, cumin or nigella seeds instead of poppy seeds, or a mixture of seeds.

Per loaf Energy 2302kcal/9787kJ; Protein 63.5g; Carbohydrate 524.5g, of which sugars 10.1g; Fat 8.8g, of which saturates 1.3g; Cholesterol 0mg; Calcium 946mg; Fibre 20.9g; Sodium 3950mg.

Sugar shortbread rounds

Shortbread should always be in the biscuit tin or cookie jar – it is so moreish. Serve these melting buttery biscuits with a cup of tea or with fruit fools or junket. A traditional Scottish favourite, they can also be half-dipped into melted chocolate and left to set.

Makes about 24

450g/1lb/2 cups salted butter

225g/8oz/1 heaped cup caster (superfine) sugar

450g/1lb/4 cups plain (all-purpose) flour

225g/8oz/scant 1½ cups ground rice or rice flour

5ml/1 tsp salt

demerara (raw) sugar, to decorate

golden caster (superfine) sugar, for dusting

Cook's tip Rice flour adds a grittiness to the dough, distinguishing home-made shortbread from bought varieties.

1 Preheat the oven to 190°C/375°F/ Gas 5. Make sure all the ingredients are at room temperature. Salted butter has more flavour than unsalted (sweet), but if you only have unsalted, then use it – don't make a special trip to the shops to buy some.

2 In a food processor or bowl, cream the butter and sugar together until light, pale and fluffy. If you used a food processor, scrape the mixture out into a mixing bowl.

3 Sift together the flour, ground rice or rice flour and salt and stir into the butter and sugar with a wooden spoon, until the mixture resembles fine breadcrumbs.

4 Working quickly, gather the dough together with your hand, then put it on a clean work surface. Knead lightly together until it forms a ball but take care not to over-knead or the shortbread will be tough and greasy. Lightly roll into a sausage shape, about 7.5cm/3in thick. Wrap in clear film (plastic wrap) and chill until firm.

5 Pour the demerara sugar on to a sheet of baking parchment. Unwrap the dough and roll in the sugar until evenly coated. Slice the roll into discs about 1cm/½in thick.

6 Place the discs on to two baking sheets lined with baking parchment, spacing well apart. Bake for 20–25 minutes until very pale gold (but not dark).

7 Remove from the oven and sprinkle with golden caster sugar. Allow to cool for 10 minutes before transferring to a wire rack to cool completely.

Per portion Energy 275kcal/1147kJ; Protein 2.5g; Carbohydrate 32g, of which sugars 10.2g; Fat 15.7g, of which saturates 9.8g; Cholesterol 40mg; Calcium 37mg; Fibre 0.8g; Sodium 197mg.

Cherry melting moments

As the name suggests, these crisp biscuits really do melt in the mouth. They have a texture like shortbread but are covered in rolled oats to give a crunchy surface and extra flavour. They are traditionally topped with a toothsome nugget of red glacé cherry.

Makes about 16–20

40g/1½oz/3 tbsp soft butter

65g/2½oz/5 tbsp lard

75g/3oz/6 tbsp caster (superfine) sugar

1 egg yolk, beaten

few drops of vanilla or almond extract

150g/5oz/1¼ cups self-raising (self-rising) flour

rolled oats, for coating

4–5 glacé (candied) cherries

3 Spread rolled oats on a sheet of baking parchment and toss the balls in them until evenly coated.

4 Place the balls, spaced slightly apart, on two baking (cookie) sheets. Flatten each ball a little with your thumb. Cut the cherries into quarters and place a piece of cherry on top of each biscuit (cookie). Put into the hot oven and cook for 15–20 minutes, until they are lightly browned.

5 Allow the biscuits to cool for a few minutes on the baking sheets before transferring them to a wire rack to cool completely.

1 Preheat the oven to 180°C/350°F/ Gas 4. Beat together the butter, lard and sugar, then gradually beat in the egg yolk and vanilla or almond extract.

2 Sift the flour over and stir to make a soft dough. Roll into 16–20 small balls.

Per portion Energy 88kcal/370kJ; Protein 0.7g; Carbohydrate 10.9g, of which sugars 5.4g; Fat 5g, of which saturates 2.4g; Cholesterol 7mg; Calcium 30mg; Fibre 0.3g; Sodium 40mg.

Porridge biscuits

Nutritious, delicious and chewy, oats are a major ingredient in these traditional country biscuits. They are store-cupboard standbys, and you can embellish the recipe by adding whichever varieties of chopped nuts, dried fruits or seeds you have to hand.

Makes about 18

115g/4oz/½ cup butter

115g/4oz/½ cup soft brown sugar

115g/4oz/½ cup golden (light corn) syrup

150g/5oz/1¼ cups self-raising (self-rising) flour

150g/5oz rolled porridge oats

1 Preheat the oven to 180°C/350°F/Gas 4. Line two baking (cookie) sheets with baking parchment, or grease with butter.

2 Gently heat the butter, sugar and golden syrup until the butter has melted and the sugar has dissolved. Remove from the heat and leave to cool slightly.

3 Sift the flour and stir into the mixture in the pan, together with the oats, to make a soft dough.

4 Roll the dough into small balls and arrange them on the prepared baking sheets, leaving plenty of room for them to spread. Flatten each ball slightly with a palette knife or a metal spatula.

5 Put one tray into the hot oven and cook for 12–15 minutes until golden brown and cooked through.

6 Leave to cool on the baking sheet for 1–2 minutes, then carefully transfer to a wire rack to crisp up and cool completely, while you cook the remaining batches.

Variation Add 25g/1oz/¼ cup chopped toasted almonds or walnuts, or a small handful of dried fruit, such as raisins, sultanas (golden raisins), chopped dried figs, dates or apricots, in step 3.

Per portion Energy 151kcal/637kJ; Protein 1.8g; Carbohydrate 23.9g, of which sugars 11.9g; Fat 6g, of which saturates 3.3g; Cholesterol 14mg; Calcium 22mg; Fibre 0.8g; Sodium 59mg.

Ginger biscuits

These crisp little biscuits are very versatile. You can cut them into any shape – but stars and hearts are the traditional forms – and they can also be decorated with icing. They are good served with ice cream or as part of a selection of biscuits for cheese.

Makes about 50

150g/5½oz/½ cup plus
3 tbsp butter

400g/14oz/2 cups sugar

50ml/2fl oz/¼ cup golden
(light corn) syrup

15ml/1 tbsp treacle (molasses)

15ml/1 tbsp ground ginger

30ml/2 tbsp ground cinnamon

15ml/1 tbsp ground cloves

5ml/1 tsp ground cardamom

5ml/1 tsp bicarbonate of soda
(baking soda)

250ml/8fl oz/1 cup water

150g/5oz/1¼ cups plain
(all-purpose) flour

1 Put the butter, sugar, syrup, treacle, ginger, cinnamon, cloves and cardamom in a heavy pan and heat gently until the butter has melted.

2 Put the bicarbonate of soda and water in a large heatproof bowl. Pour in the warm spice mixture and mix well together, then add the flour and stir until well blended. Wrap in clear film (plastic wrap) and put in the refrigerator overnight to rest.

3 Preheat the oven to 220°C/425°F/ Gas 7. Line several baking sheets with baking parchment. Knead the dough, then roll out on a lightly floured surface as thinly as possible. Cut the dough into shapes of your choice and place on the baking sheets.

4 Bake the biscuits (cookies) in the oven for about 5 minutes until golden brown, adding them in batches until all the biscuits are cooked. Leave to cool on the baking sheet. Make sure the biscuits are completely cold before icing or decorating them.

Per portion Energy 31kcal/130kJ; Protein 0.2g; Carbohydrate 5.8g, of which sugars 4.2g; Fat 0.8g, of which saturates 0.5g; Cholesterol 2mg; Calcium 5mg; Fibre 0.1g; Sodium13mg.

Honey cake

The type of honey you choose affects the flavour of this cake. Use a darker honey in the recipe, then drizzle over a flower honey such as orange blossom while the cake is still warm.

Makes 16 squares

175g/6oz/¾ cup butter

175g/6oz/¾ cup clear honey

115g/4oz/½ cup soft brown sugar

2 eggs, lightly beaten

15–30ml/1–2 tbsp milk

225g/8oz/2 cups self-raising (self-rising) flour

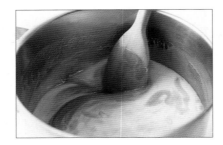

3 Beat the eggs and milk into the cooled mixture. Sift the flour over the top, stir in and beat well until smooth.

4 Place the mixture into the prepared tin, levelling the surface. Put into the hot oven and cook for about 30 minutes until well risen, golden brown and firm to the touch.

5 Leave the cake to cool in the tin for 20 minutes, then turn out, leaving the lining paper in place, on to a wire rack and leave to cool completely.

6 Peel off the paper and cut the cake into 16 squares. Serve with drizzled honey.

1 Grease and line a 23cm/9in square cake tin (pan) with baking parchment. Preheat the oven to 180°C/350°F/Gas 4.

2 Gently heat the butter, honey and sugar, stirring frequently until well amalgamated. Set aside and leave to cool slightly.

Variation Add 5ml/1 tsp ground cinnamon or grated nutmeg to the flour in step 3.

Per portion Energy 152kcal/639kJ; Protein 1.9g; Carbohydrate 23.5g, of which sugars 13g; Fat 6.3g, of which saturates 3.8g; Cholesterol 26mg; Calcium 30mg; Fibre 0.4g; Sodium 49mg

Blueberry muffins

Light and fluffy, muffins are best eaten fresh for breakfast or brunch. Add some chopped
pecans or walnuts for extra crunch, or replace the blueberries with fresh cranberries.

Makes 12

180g/6¼oz/generous 1½ cups
plain (all-purpose) flour

60g/2¼oz/generous ¼ cup sugar

10ml/2 tsp baking powder

1.5ml/¼ tsp salt

2 eggs

50g/2oz/4 tbsp butter, melted

175ml/6fl oz/¾ cup milk

5ml/1 tsp vanilla extract

5ml/1 tsp grated lemon rind

175g/6oz/1½ cups fresh
blueberries

1 Preheat the oven to 200°C/400°F/
Gas 6. Grease a 12-cup muffin tin (pan)
or arrange 12 paper muffin cases on
a baking tray.

2 Sift the flour, sugar, baking powder
and salt into a large mixing bowl. In
another bowl, whisk the eggs until
blended. Add the melted butter, milk,
vanilla and lemon rind to the eggs,
and stir thoroughly to combine.

5 Spoon the batter into the muffin tin
or paper cases, leaving enough room
for the muffins to rise.

6 Bake for 20–25 minutes, until the
tops spring back when touched lightly.
Leave the muffins in the tin, if using, for
5 minutes before turning out on to a
wire rack to cool a little before serving.

3 Make a well in the dry ingredients
and pour in the egg mixture. With a
large metal spoon, stir until the flour
is just moistened, but not smooth.

4 Add the blueberries to the muffin
mixture and gently fold in, being
careful not to crush any of the berries
while you stir them.

Cook's tip If you want to serve
these muffins for breakfast, prepare
the dry ingredients the night before
to save time.

Per portion Energy 236kcal/992kJ; Protein 4.9g; Carbohydrate 34.7g, of which sugars 12.4g; Fat 9.6g, of which saturates 5.6g; Cholesterol 54mg; Calcium 88mg; Fibre 1.4g; Sodium 82mg.

Plum and almond sponge cake

Seasonal country cooking is an obvious necessity in cold areas that have fierce extremes of climate. Traditionally, people ate what they could grow and stored food carefully to survive until the next harvest. Orchards have always been especially prized, and apple, pear and plum trees thrive in many cold countries. These fruits add sweetness, texture and variety to cakes. This sponge is best served warm and is equally good made with apricots or nectarines. The cardamom gives a hint of spice, which complements the fruit perfectly.

Serves 10

450g/1lb pitted fresh plums, coarsely chopped, plus 9 extra plums, stoned and halved, to decorate

300ml/½ pint/1¼ cups water

115g/4oz/½ cup unsalted (sweet) butter, softened

200g/7oz/1 cup caster (superfine) sugar

3 eggs

90g/3½oz/¾ cup toasted, finely chopped almonds

5ml/1 tsp bicarbonate of soda (baking soda)

7.5ml/1½ tsp baking powder

5ml/1 tsp ground cardamom

1.5ml/¼ tsp salt

250g/9oz/2¼ cups plain (all-purpose) flour

15ml/1 tbsp pearl sugar, to decorate

250ml/8fl oz/1 cup double (heavy) cream

10ml/2 tsp vanilla sugar

10ml/2 tsp icing (confectioners') sugar

Variation Pearl sugar – large crystals with a pearly sheen – is commonly used in Scandinavia to decorate pastries, buns and cakes. If you can't find it, use coarsely crushed white sugar cubes.

1 Place the chopped plums in a pan and add the water. Bring to the boil over a medium heat and cook for 10–15 minutes, until soft. Set aside to cool. You will need 350ml/12fl oz/1½ cups stewed plums for the cake.

2 Preheat the oven to 180°C/350°F/ Gas 4. Grease and flour a 24cm/9½in springform cake tin (pan).

3 Cream the butter with the sugar in a mixing bowl until light and fluffy. Beat in the eggs, one at a time.

4 Stir in the stewed plums and the almonds. Add the baking soda, baking powder, cardamom and salt, and stir the mixture well together to distribute the fruit.

5 Gradually stir in the flour, a few spoons at a time, and mix until blended.

6 Pour the mixture into the prepared tin. Place 15 plum halves around the circumference of the cake and the remaining three halves in the centre, cut sides down. Sprinkle the pearl sugar over the cake.

7 Bake for 1 hour, or until the top springs back when lightly touched. Cool in the tin for 15 minutes before unfastening the ring.

8 Beat the double cream until soft peaks form. Stir in the vanilla sugar and the icing sugar and beat until thick. Serve the cake, still slightly warm, or at room temperature, in slices topped with a dollop of whipped cream.

Per portion Energy 311kcal/1308kJ; Protein 6.4g; Carbohydrate 44.5g, of which sugars 15.9g; Fat 13.2g, of which saturates 7.4g; Cholesterol 89mg; Calcium 86mg; Fibre 2.4g; Sodium 102mg.

Preserves, relishes and sauces

As well as preserving the taste of summer fruits and vegetables, it is immensely satisfying to make your own jams, jellies and relishes. Country-style home-made ones always taste better than store-bought varieties, and also make lovely gifts. Spicy and fruity sauces enliven the simplest of rustic dishes, and stirring a bubbling pot of preserves is a highly pleasurable rural pastime – both easy and rewarding.

Cherry berry conserve

Tart cranberries add an extra dimension to this delicious berry conserve. It is perfect for adding to sweet sauces, serving with roast duck, or for simply spreading on hot crumpets.

1 Put the cranberries in a food processor and process until coarsely chopped. Scrape into a pan and add the cherries, fruit syrup and lemon juice.

2 Add the water to the pan. Cover and bring to the boil, then simmer for 20–30 minutes, until the cranberries are tender.

3 Add the sugar to the pan and heat gently, stirring, until the sugar has dissolved. Bring to the boil, then cook for 10 minutes, or to setting point (105°C/220°F).

4 Remove the pan from the heat and skim off and discard any scum using a slotted spoon. Leave to cool for 10 minutes, then stir gently and pour into warmed sterilized jars. Seal, label and store in a cool, dark place.

Cook's tip The cranberries must be cooked until very tender before the sugar is added, otherwise they will become tough.

Makes about 1.3kg/3lb

350g/12oz/3 cups fresh cranberries

1kg/2¼lb/5½ cups cherries, pitted

120ml/4fl oz/½ cup blackcurrant or raspberry syrup

juice of 2 lemons

250ml/8fl oz/1 cup water

1.3kg/3lb/6½ cups preserving or granulated (white) sugar, warmed

Per portion Energy 5859kcal/24,986kJ; Protein 16.7g; Carbohydrate 1540.4g, of which sugars 1540.4g; Fat 1.4g, of which saturates 0g; Cholesterol 0mg; Calcium 844mg; Fibre 14.6g; Sodium 105mg.

Hedgerow jelly

In the autumn, foraged hedgerow fruits such as damsons, blackberries and elderberries are wonderful for this delightful country jelly. Serve with cold meats or cheese.

Makes about 1.3kg/3lb

450g/1lb damsons, washed

450g/1lb/4 cups
blackberries, washed

225g/8oz/2 cups raspberries

225g/8oz/2 cups
elderberries, washed

juice and pips (seeds) of
2 large lemons

about 1.3kg/3lb/6½ cups
preserving or granulated
(white) sugar, warmed

3 Measure the strained juice into a preserving pan. Add 450g/1lb/ 2¼ cups sugar for every 600ml/ 1 pint/2½ cups strained fruit juice.

4 Heat the mixture, stirring, over a low heat until the sugar has dissolved.

5 Increase the heat and boil rapidly without stirring for 10–15 minutes, or until the jelly reaches setting point (105°C/220°F).

6 Remove the pan from the heat and skim off any scum using a slotted spoon.

7 Ladle into warmed, sterilized jars and seal. Leave to cool, then label and store for up to 6 months.

1 Put the fruit, lemon juice and pips in a large pan. Add water to just below the level of the fruit. Cover and simmer for 1 hour. Mash the fruit, then leave to cool slightly.

2 Pour into a scalded jelly bag suspended over a non-metallic bowl and leave to drain overnight. Don't squeeze the bag as this will cloud the jelly.

Per portion Energy 5229kcal/22,306kJ; Protein 9.3g; Carbohydrate 1382.8g, of which sugars 1382.8g; Fat 0.4g, of which saturates 0g; Cholesterol 0mg; Calcium 799mg; Fibre 8.6g; Sodium 86mg.

Pickled spiced red cabbage

This delicately spiced and vibrant-coloured pickle is an old-fashioned favourite to serve with bread and cheese for an informal lunch, or to accompany pies, terrines or cold cuts.

Makes about 1–1.6kg/2¼–3½lb

675g/1½lb/6 cups red cabbage, shredded

1 large Spanish (Bermuda) onion, sliced

30ml/2 tbsp sea salt

600ml/1 pint/2½ cups red wine vinegar

75g/3oz/6 tbsp light muscovado (brown) sugar

15ml/1 tbsp coriander seeds

3 cloves

2.5cm/1in piece fresh root ginger

1 whole star anise

2 bay leaves

4 eating apples

1 Put the cabbage and onion in a bowl, add the salt and mix well until thoroughly combined.

2 Transfer the mixture into a colander over a bowl and leave to drain overnight.

3 The next day, rinse the salted vegetables, drain well and pat dry using kitchen paper. Transfer them to a colander.

4 Pour the vinegar into a pan, add the sugar, spices and bay leaves and boil. Remove from the heat and leave to cool.

5 Core and chop the apples, then layer with the cabbage and onions in sterilized preserving jars. Pour over the cooled spiced vinegar. Seal the jars and store for 1 week before eating. Eat within 2 months. Once opened, store in the refrigerator.

Per portion Energy 674kcal/2868kJ; Protein 12g; Carbohydrate 161.4g, of which sugars 159.3g; Fat 2g, of which saturates 0g; Cholesterol 0mg; Calcium 405mg; Fibre 23g; Sodium 64mg.

Traditional pickled onions

Essential for a ploughman's lunch, pickled onions should be crunchy and pungent, and stored for at least six weeks for the flavours to develop. Try making some for Christmas.

Makes about 4 jars

1kg/2¼lb pickling (pearl) onions

115g/4oz/½ cup salt

750ml/1¼ pints/3 cups malt vinegar

15ml/1 tbsp sugar

2–3 dried red chillies

5ml/1 tsp brown mustard seeds

15ml/1 tbsp coriander seeds

5ml/1 tsp allspice berries

5ml/1 tsp black peppercorns

5cm/2in piece fresh root ginger, sliced

2–3 blades mace

2–3 fresh bay leaves

1 To peel the onions, trim off the root ends, but leave the onion layers attached. Cut a thin slice off the top (neck) end of the onion. Place the onions in a bowl, then cover with boiling water. Leave to stand for about 4 minutes, then drain. The skin should then be easy to peel using a small, sharp knife.

2 Place the peeled onions in a bowl and cover with cold water, then drain the water into a large pan. Add the salt and heat slightly to dissolve it, then cool before pouring the brine over the onions.

3 Place a plate inside the top of the bowl and weigh it down slightly so that it keeps all the onions submerged in the brine. Leave to stand for 24 hours.

4 Meanwhile, place the vinegar in a large pan. Wrap all the remaining ingredients, except the bay leaves, in a piece of muslin (cheesecloth). Bring to the boil, simmer for about 5 minutes, then remove the pan from the heat. Set aside, cover and leave in a cool place overnight to infuse.

5 The next day, drain the onions, rinse and pat dry. Pack them into sterilized 450g/1lb jars. Add some or all of the spice from the vinegar, except the ginger slices. The pickle will become hotter if you add the chillies. Pour the vinegar over to cover and add the bay leaves. (Store leftover vinegar in a bottle for another batch of pickles.)

6 Seal the jars with non-metallic lids and store in a cool, dark place for at least 6 weeks before eating.

Per portion Energy 109kcal/454kJ; Protein 3.1g; Carbohydrate 24.5g, of which sugars 18.6g; Fat 0.5g, of which saturates 0g; Cholesterol 0mg; Calcium 67mg; Fibre 3.6g; Sodium 8mg.

Mint sauce

In England, mint sauce is the traditional and inseparable accompaniment to roast lamb. Its fresh tart and astringent flavour is the perfect foil to rich, strongly flavoured lamb. As well as being extremely simple to make, it is infinitely superior to the store-bought varieties.

Makes about 250ml/8fl oz/1cup

1 large bunch mint

105ml/7 tbsp boiling water

150ml/¼ pint/⅔ cup wine vinegar

30ml/2 tbsp granulated (white) sugar

Cook's tip To make a quick and speedy Indian raita for serving with crispy poppadums, simply stir a little mint sauce into a small bowl of natural (plain) yogurt. Serve the raita alongside a bowl of tangy mango chutney.

1 Using a sharp knife, chop the mint very finely and place it in a 600ml/ 1 pint/2½ cup jug (pitcher). Pour the boiling water over the mint and leave to infuse for about 10 minutes.

2 When the mint infusion has cooled and is lukewarm, stir in the wine vinegar and sugar. Continue stirring (but do not mash up the mint leaves) until the sugar has dissolved completely.

3 Pour the mint sauce into a warmed sterilized bottle or jar. Seal the jar, label it with the date and store in the refrigerator or a cool, dark place.

Cook's tip This mint sauce can keep for up to 6 months when stored in the refrigerator, but is best when used within 3 weeks.

Per portion Energy 161kcal/685kJ; Protein 3.9g; Carbohydrate 36.6g, of which sugars 31.3g; Fat 0.7g, of which saturates 0g; Cholesterol 0mg; Calcium 226mg; Fibre 0g; Sodium 17mg.

Real horseradish sauce

Fiery, peppery horseradish sauce is without doubt the essential accompaniment to roast beef, and is also delicious served with smoked salmon. Horseradish, like chilli, is a powerful ingredient, so take care when handling it, and always wash your hands afterwards.

Makes about 200ml/7fl oz/scant 1 cup

45ml/3 tbsp freshly grated horseradish root

15ml/1 tbsp white wine vinegar

5ml/1 tsp granulated (white) sugar

pinch of salt

150ml/¼ pint/⅔ cup thick double (heavy) cream, for serving

Cook's tip To counteract the potent fumes of the horseradish, keep the root submerged in water while you chop and peel it. Use a food processor to do the fine chopping or grating, and avert your head when removing the lid.

1 Place the grated horseradish in a bowl, then add the white wine vinegar, granulated sugar and just a pinch of salt.

2 Stir the ingredients together, mixing them well until they are thoroughly combined and smooth.

3 Pour the mixture into a sterilized jar. It will keep in the refrigerator for up to 6 months.

4 A few hours before you intend to serve the sauce, stir the cream into the horseradish and leave to infuse. Stir once again before serving.

Per portion Energy 774kcal/3190kJ; Protein 2.8g; Carbohydrate 9.9g, of which sugars 9.8g; Fat 80.7g, of which saturates 50.1g; Cholesterol 206mg; Calcium 98mg; Fibre 1.1g; Sodium 40mg.

Index